P9-CJM-063

"The general feeling, at this stage, was
that an air strike against the missile sites
could be the only course. Listening to the
proposals, I passed a note to the President: 'I now know how Tojo felt when
he was planning Pearl Harbor.' "
—Robert F. Kennedy

"Everything was going to work out satisfactorily . . . I went back to the White
House and talked to the President for a
long time. As I was leaving, he said,
making reference to Abraham Lincoln,
'This is the night I should go to the
theatre.' I said, 'If you go, I want to go
with you.' "
—Robert F. Kennedy

Other MENTOR and SIGNET Books
of Special Interest

This new anthology is a stimulating collection of poetic expression that provides an opportunity to examine what women have been thinking and feeling for the last century. Because representation in most of the poetry anthologies of the past has not gone beyond tokenism, most women writers have remained minor figures in the male-dominated literary world. This book is an attempt to make both men and women aware of the vital force women poets today represent.

A short biography and a picture accompany the work of each poet.

RISING TIDES

20th Century American Women Poets

edited by

Laura Chester

and

Sharon Barba

A KANGAROO BOOK
PUBLISHED BY POCKET BOOKS NEW YORK

RISING TIDES: 20th Century American Women Poets

WASHINGTON SQUARE PRESS edition published July, 1973

Published by
POCKET BOOKS, a Simon & Schuster Division of
GULF & WESTERN CORPORATION
1230 Avenue of the Americas, New York, N.Y. 10020.

WASHINGTON SQUARE PRESS editions are distributed in
the U.S. by Simon & Schuster, Inc., 1230 Avenue of the
Americas, New York, N.Y. 10020, and in Canada by Simon
& Schuster of Canada, Ltd., Markham, Ontario, Canada.

ACKNOWLEDGMENTS AND COPYRIGHT NOTICES

Editor; "Clearing the Air" and "Marriage Amulet," printe[d] by permission of the author.

HELEN WOLFERT: the selection from "Woman Against the Moon," appearing originally in *The American Poet*, copyright 194[ ] by James Meagher, reprinted by permission of the author[.] "The Cat" and "The Grass" from *The Music Poems*, copy[-]right © 1965 by Helen Wolfert, reprinted by permission o[f] W. W. Norton & Company, Inc.

ELINOR WYLIE: "Wild Peaches," copyright 1921 by Alfred A[.] Knopf, Inc. and renewed 1949 by William Rose Benet, an[d] "Prophecy," copyright 1923 by Alfred A. Knopf, Inc., bot[h] from *Collected Poems of Elinor Wylie* and reprinted b[y] permission of Alfred A. Knopf, Inc.

NOTE: The editors regret the omission of several poets whose work merits inclusion in this anthology. Due to the nature of this book, Elizabeth Bishop, Gwendolyn Brooks, Diane Wakoski, and Jean Valentine did not wish to be represented.

The editors' special thanks go to Laurie Brown at Washington Square Press.

CONTENTS

CONTENTS · xix

From the Editors

In the twentieth century, a growing number of wom-
 poets are writing, and their work merits attention.
he significant number of poets is important, but our
 ncern is also with the richness and independence
 at these voices offer. Because of the poems and poets
 cluded here, we feel that this book will prove to be more
 an a "timely" and soon-to-be-dated collection; it will
 nd as evidence that this century marks the beginning of
 poetic renaissance for women.

Today a few women are well known in contemporary
 etry, and an increasing number are being published; but
 e work of many talented women writers has not been
 cognized or widely anthologized, and, therefore, is not
 cessible to a large audience. For the most part, the
 resentation of women in anthologies has not gone far
 yond tokenism. Within a changing society and a chang-
 literature, archaic attitudes toward women, and wom-
 writers specifically, persist. We hope that this book will
 p dispel these limitations.

There continues to be an underlying social objection to
 men writing at all, although most people today would
 embarrassed to proclaim that a woman's place is in the
 me. As Elaine Showalter, a contemporary feminist critic,
 s in the Introduction to *Women's Liberation and Lit-
 ture,* "Women have always encountered more critical
 stance than men . . . primarily because literary cre-
 ity has seemed to rival biological creativity in the most
 ct way." We are still not so far from thinking that a
 man should only make babies and casseroles, rather
 books, and that the woman who chooses books is
 a Real Woman.

Women persist in writing anyway, but they are oft
regarded as a kind of ladies' auxiliary of literature, ma
ing at best what is regarded as sub-literature, an imitati
of male work. Thus the first criticism of women writers
that they are not men. As Hortense Calisher says in b
article "No Important Woman Writer," there exists
usually unspoken assumption that major art is by a
about men (or male activities, which includes women).

Such thinking allows John Crowe Ransom to conclu
his discussion of Edna St. Vincent Millay in *The Worl*
Body by saying "that women, like children, just can't wr
good poetry because they never really grow up": mean
that they do not grow up to be men. It allows an editor
a small poetry press to tell a young woman poet, in su
posed sympathy for her work, that women are hamper
because they do not have their own whore houses a
cannot ship out to sea. The experiences of women are h
to be narrow and unimportant compared to those of m
unsuitable for literature.

Should these "arguments" fail to seem convincing, th
are men who contend that genius itself is a male attrib
and that women accordingly will never produce gr
literature: i.e., where is the female Shakespeare? Anyo
seriously interested in that question should remember V
ginia Woolf's *A Room of One's Own*. Woolf knows t
genius does not develop and articulate itself in a vacu
or against every form of opposition, that its expression a
fulfillment is dependent partly upon social conditions.
need to maintain an historical perspective in relation
women today.

Consider the conditions of women's lives in a patriarc
culture, the attitudes of a male society toward women, a
the fact that a subordinate group internalizes much of
thinking of the dominant group about its own nature.
Erica Jong puts it in "Alcestis on the Poetry Circuit"

> The best slave
> does not need to be beaten.
> She beats herself.

nsider not only the lack of encouragement but the ac-
e discouragement that most women have encountered
en they wished to move beyond their prescribed roles.
nsider the lack of education formerly available to wom-
 in the male culture. By definition, illiterates do not
ke literature. Just as the original feminist movement in
 nineteenth century was begun by America's first group
 women to graduate from college, it is no coincidence
 t the majority of women poets in the twentieth century
ve had a higher education and are moving into new
es previously denied them.

The increase in the number of genuine poets among
men is linked directly to the improvement in the "con-
ion of women" in this century. As Woolf says in *A
om of One's Own,*

nasterpieces are not single and solitary births; they
 ire the outcome of many years of thinking in com-
non, of thinking by the body of the people, so that
 he experience of the mass is behind the single voice.

ne may object to what they see as the reduction of
 rature to a social phenomenon, to our saying that the
 etus behind this book is social in the broadest sense.
 believe that our lives seen through poetry will give
 ght into the predicaments women (and therefore men)
 st face today, insights that have their genesis in a per-
 al and aesthetic response, reflecting the fluid condition
 our culture. We feel that these poems will illuminate a
 mon ground for those of many different orientations
 attitudes. The danger is in listening to those who
 ntain that we are confusing literature and life, as
 ugh there were no connection at all between them.
 ome of the poems included here, and some of the
 nger poets in particular, might be called distinctly
 inist. But defined in the largest sense, feminism is
 ply a belief in the full humanity of woman and her
 t to define herself. When we are told to think of our-
 es as persons rather than as women, we are usually being
 to act, or write, like men. When we attempt to forget

our sex, we become what Germaine Greer has so apt
called the female eunuch. We have overlooked whatev
is good in our sex; we have learned not to value ourselv
as women.

Must we believe that the only way to praise a wom
writer is to say that she is unlike the other members of h
sex, that she is no typical woman writer (or the cri
wouldn't be wasting his time)? The danger for wom
writers is not that they will be "too feminine," but th
they will attempt to disregard their femininity. As Calish
continues,

> the American artist has sometimes avoided [her fem-
> ininity], by getting her mental hysterectomy early.
> She will often not speak for female experience even
> when the men do. She will be the angel-artist, with
> celestially muted lower parts. Sometimes, in any of
> the arts, where women's work remains beautifully
> mandarin or minor, it may be not because of their
> womanhood but from their lack of it.

Women must learn the self-love, the self-idealizing,
self-mythologizing, that has made it possible for men
think of themselves as persons. The first step is to ackno
edge that one is a woman and to begin discovering w
that may mean. These poems show that discovery tak
place. Most of the poems we have chosen—and we fou
this kind of poem in the work of every woman we read
may be called "poems about women." They are poe
which speak with a woman's voice, through a woma
perceptions, about a woman's experiences; they refl
what may be called a feminine consciousness.

We believe that any human being ought to be interes
in what Carolyn Kizer in "Pro Femina" calls "the wor
best kept secret: merely, the private lives of one-half
humanity." We believe that just as literature reflects
lives of those who make it, so in turn it affects social
titudes: literature can aid in changing the image of w
en. In poetry, women have served as subject matter
"inspiration" for male poets; it is time to listen to wor

emselves, to discover new angles of perception on the
bject, new images.

We may, by writing as women, discover something about
rselves as persons, about the world, and about art, that
en have never seen. For the culture as a whole, we be-
ve that unless it accepts at last the feminine in itself,
comes genuinely androgynous, it is doomed to what we
all indulge ourselves here by calling impotency. In the
ts, and in literature specifically, the influence of women
n only be vitalizing.

LAURA CHESTER
SHARON BARBA

Carolynn Fischel

Introduction

Jean Cocteau said that poetry was indispensable, but he
did not know why. This anthology may answer the question, for every mood, every experience, every aspect of
the world, demands expression, and here we might turn
casually to any page, and find the words we need for in-
dignation, anger, injustice, love, passion, religious and
pagan prayers, cries of distress and cries of joy. We can
turn to it on blank days when either our sorrows or our
joys do not find their voice. So many poets are gathered
here together to voice the entire range of human experience, in every variation of voice and tone, employing every
color and every texture, every level of talk, from meta-
morphosis to plain and homely untransfigured statements.
Poetry is no longer to be defined as of old; it has opened
its doors to direct statements, to slogans, to marching
songs, to hymns and to street songs. It is no longer a
solitary chant; it has become common to all and inclusive
of all races, religions and irreligions. The variety of levels
and themes makes these poems universal, but this poetry
also focuses on revelations of women which need to be
heard. Ultimately this poetry, this anthology, is the song
of women.
My own definition of the poet is one who teaches us
levitation, because I feel poetry is needed to lift us above
despair, and above our human condition, so we may become aware that we need not be overwhelmed by the
weight of earth, the ponderous oppression of quotidian
burdens. The burdens here are dwelt upon; poetry in this
anthology is not only the transformer or the indicator to
other forms of life. It is the poetry of today, and the poetry
of woman at a crucial period of evolution. The selection is

wide. It will place poetry as a daily necessity, as a nourish
ment, as useful to the community, the equivalent of ou
daily speech, our daily thoughts and feelings. In this wa
it may prove its indispensable quality. In the terms
Gaston Bachelard, the poet philosopher and philosoph
of poetry, we have here the poetics of fire, space, earth, a
and water.

Gaston Bachelard writes that "poetry gives us maste
of our tongue." And only by this mastery can we ma
ourselves understood by others, and make our needs, o
demands, our predicaments, our dilemmas, known.

He also writes: "There is no need to have lived throu
the poet's suffering in order to seize the felicity that do
inates tragedy itself." And: "To mount too high, or
scend too low, is allowed in the case of the poet who bri
earth and sky together."

Poets help us to see more, to hear more, to disco
within ourselves such landscapes, such emotions, su
reveries, such relationships to people, to nature, to
perience, as may remain unknown to us before they
scribe it, for to sustain our dreams and our lover's nee
we need to absorb from poets their capacity for seeing a
hearing what daily life obscures from us.

Two kinds of space, intimate and outer, struggle for
attention, and struggle for integration, for in integrat
and fusion lies the power of ecstasy which enables us
conquer despair and conquer human oppression.

Rilke said: "The plain is the sentiment which ex
us." But the description of the not plain is what sust
us in our search; the description of the marvelous state
consciousness attainable is what propels us upward rat
than downward.

Poetry, no matter what its subject, can propel us
ward, for it gives to our most ordinary experience the g
of a tale, the illumination of myth, the song's contagi
rhythm, a troubadour's romance.

Gaston Bachelard again: "Any sentiment that exalt
makes our situation in the world smoother."

When history, when our world becomes intolerable,
young turn to poetry. They write enormous amounts

ey sing it, they print it themselves. It is the creative drug, e creative painkiller, the creative tranquilizer, the cre- ve healer.

This is an era of poetry, poetry against the inarticulate, e stuttering, the muttering wordless suffering which can- t be shared or heard. The skillful, the clarified expres- n of our joys and sorrows, our angers and rebellions, kes them sharable and therefore less destructive. Words exorcism of pain, indispensable to communion, the op- site of war.

The fusion here is in the voice of woman. Woman termined to end woman's mysteries and woman's secrets. e need to know her better. Let us approach her and en to her in these condensed, in these concentrated and tilled messages, to become intimate with her.

It is not only the Oriental woman who wore veils. There psychic veils, and these are best lifted by poets, so we acquire from them at the same time their constant iscovery of love.

ANAÏS NIN

I am obnoxious to each carping tongue
Who says my hand a needle better fits;
A poet's pen all scorn I should thus wrong,
For such despite they cast on female wits.
If what I do prove well, it won't advance;
They'll say it's stol'n, or else it was by chance.

Anne Bradstreet
from "The Prologue," 1650

The blood jet is poetry,
There is no stopping it.

Sylvia Plath
from "Kindness," 1962

RISING TIDES

20th Century American Women Poets

Ida Williams Pritchett

GERTRUDE STEIN was born February 3, 1874 in Allegheny, Pennsylvania. She studied psychology with William James at Radcliffe, and medicine at Johns Hopkins; she left Johns Hopkins shortly before she would have received her degree, having refused to take the examinations because, as she said, medicine was "boring." After 1903 she lived in Paris, first with her brother Leo and then with Alice B. Toklas. Her apartment was a constant gathering place for artists, including Picasso, Apollinaire, and Hemingway. She died in France in 1946. Some of her works include *Three Lives* (1909), *The Making of Americans* (written by 1908 but not published until 1925), *Tender Buttons* (1914), *Lucy Church Amiably* (1930), *The Autobiography of Alice B. Toklas* (1933), and *Lectures in America* (1935). Her other work includes operas, portraits, and writing on World War II. Carl Van Vechten edited her late and unpublished writing.

1

STORYETTE H. M.

One was married to some one. That one was going a⟨
to have a good time. The one that was married to that
did not like it very well that the one to whom that one ⟨
married then was going off alone to have a good time ⟨
was leaving that one to stay at home then. The one ⟨
was going came in all glowing. The one that was g⟨
had everything he was needing to have the good time ⟨
was wanting to be having then. He came in all glow⟨
The one he was leaving at home to take care of the fa⟨
living was not glowing. The one that was going was say⟨
the one that was glowing, the one that was going
saying then, I am content, you are not content, I ⟨
content, you are not content, I am content, you are cont⟨
you are content, I am content.

From: TENDER BUTTONS

A Blue Coat

A blue coat is guided guided away, guided and gui⟨
away, that is the particular color that is used for that le⟨
and not any width not even more than a shadow.

Water Raining

Water astonishing and difficult altogether make⟨
meadow and a stroke.

A Petticoat

A light white, a disgrace, an ink spot, a rosy charm.

Celery

Celery tastes tastes where in curled lashes and little
and mostly in remains.

A green acre is so selfish and so pure and so enlive⟨

Cooking

Alas, alas the pull alas the bell alas the coach in china, as the little put in leaf alas the wedding butter meat, alas e receptacle, alas the back shape of mussle, mussle and da.

Pastry

Cutting shade, cool spades and little last beds, make olet, violet when.

SUSIE ASADO

Sweet sweet sweet sweet sweet tea.
  Susie Asado.
Sweet sweet sweet sweet sweet tea.
  Susie Asado.
Susie Asado which is a told tray sure.
A lean on the shoe this means slips slips hers.
When the ancient light grey is clean it is yellow, it is a ver seller.
This is a please this is a please there are the saids to jelly. ese are the wets these say the sets to leave a crown to cy.
Incy is short for incubus.
A pot. A pot is a beginning of a rare bit of trees. Trees mble, the old vats are in bobbles, bobbles which shade d shove and render clean, render clean must.
  Drink pups.
Drink pups drink pups lease a sash hold, see it shine and obolink has pins. It shows a nail.
What is a nail. A nail is unison.
Sweet sweet sweet sweet sweet tea.

AMY LOWELL was born February 9, 1874, a
member of the famous New England Lowell family
that included James Russell Lowell. She began writing in her late twenties, and her first book, *A Dome
of Many-coloured Glass,* appeared when she was
thirty-eight. Her other volumes include *Sword Blades
and Poppy Seeds* (1914), *Men, Women and Ghosts*
(1916), *Can Grande's Castle* (1918), *Pictures of the
Floating World* (1919), *Legends* (1921), *What's
O'Clock* (1925), *East Wind* (1926), and *Ballads for
Sale* (1927). She received the Pulitzer Prize post-
humously for *What's O'Clock.* She also did translations from the Chinese, publishing *Fir-Flower
Tablets* (1921), and criticism, including *Six French
Poets* (1915), *Tendencies in Modern American
Poetry* (1917), and a biography of Keats (1925).
She had planned a biography of Emily Dickinson be-
fore her death in 1925.

4

MUSIC

The neighbour sits in his window and plays the flute.
From my bed I can hear him,
And the round notes flutter and tap about the room,
And hit against each other,
Blurring to unexpected chords.
It is very beautiful,
With the little flute-notes all about me,
In the darkness.

In the daytime,
The neighbour eats bread and onions with one hand
And copies music with the other.
He is fat and has a bald head,
So I do not look at him,
But run quickly past his window.
There is always the sky to look at,
Or the water in the well!

But when night comes and he plays his flute,
I think of him as a young man,
With gold seals hanging from his watch,
And a blue coat with silver buttons.
As I lie in my bed
The flute-notes push against my ears and lips,
And I go to sleep, dreaming.

WIND AND SILVER

Greatly shining,
The Autumn moon floats in the thin sky;
And the fish-ponds shake their backs and flash their dragon
    scales
As she passes over them.

STREETS

(Adapted from the poet Yakura Sanjin, 1769)

As I wandered through the eight hundred and eight streets
    of the city,
I saw nothing so beautiful
As the Women of the Green Houses,
With their girdles of spun gold,
And their long-sleeved dresses,
Coloured like the graining of wood.
As they walk,
The hems of their outer garments flutter open,
And the blood-red linings glow like sharp-toothed maple
    leaves
In Autumn.

A POET'S WIFE

Cho Wēn-chün to her husband Ssŭ-ma Hsiang-ju

You have taken our love and turned it into coins of silver,
You sell the love poems you wrote for me,
And with the price of them you buy many cups of wine.
I beg that you remain dumb,
That you write no more poems.
For the wine does us both an injury,
And the words of your heart
Have become the common speech of the Emperor's con-
    cubines.

MADONNA OF THE EVENING FLOWERS

All day long I have been working,
Now I am tired.
I call: "Where are you?"

But there is only the oak-tree rustling in the wind.
The house is very quiet,
The sun shines in on your books,
On your scissors and thimble just put down,
But you are not there.
Suddenly I am lonely:
Where are you?
I go about searching.

Then I see you,
Standing under a spire of pale blue larkspur,
With a basket of roses on your arm.
You are cool, like silver,
And you smile.
I think the Canterbury bells are playing little tunes.

You tell me that the peonies need spraying,
That the columbines have overrun all bounds,
That the pyrus japonica should be cut back and rounded.
You tell me these things.
But I look at you, heart of silver,
White heart-flame of polished silver,
Burning beneath the blue steeples of the larkspur,
And I long to kneel instantly at your feet,
While all about us peal the loud, sweet *Te Deums* of the
    Canterbury bells.

Nikolas Muray

ELINOR WYLIE was born Elinor Hoyt on September 7, 1885 in Somerville, New Jersey. On both sides she came from distinguished Philadelphia ancestry. She was married three times, taking her name from her second husband, and finally marrying William Rose Benét, poet and editor. She was a painter as well as a poet and novelist, and her *Collected Prose* was published in 1933. Her volumes of poetry include *Incidental Numbers* (1912), *Nets to Catch the Wind* (1921), *Black Armour* (1923), *Trivial Breath* (1928), and *Angels and Earthly Creatures* (1929). She died on December 16, 1928, and after her death her sister, Nancy Hoyt, wrote her biography.

8

WILD PEACHES

I

When the world turns completely upside down
You say we'll emigrate to the Eastern Shore
Aboard a river-boat from Baltimore;
We'll live among wild peach trees, miles from town,
You'll wear a coonskin cap, and I a gown
Homespun, dyed butternut's dark gold colour.
Lost, like your lotus-eating ancestor,
We'll swim in milk and honey till we drown.

The winter will be short, the summer long,
The autumn amber-hued, sunny and hot,
Tasting of cider and of scuppernong;
All seasons sweet, but autumn best of all.
The squirrels in their silver fur will fall
Like falling leaves, like fruit, before your shot.

2

The autumn frosts will lie upon the grass
Like bloom on grapes of purple-brown and gold.
The misted early mornings will be cold;
The little puddles will be roofed with glass.
The sun, which burns from copper into brass,
Melts these at noon, and makes the boys unfold
Their knitted mufflers; full as they can hold,
Fat pockets dribble chestnuts as they pass.

Peaches grow wild, and pigs can live in clover;
A barrel of salted herrings lasts a year;
The spring begins before the winter's over.
By February you may find the skins
Of garter snakes and water moccasins
Dwindled and harsh, dead-white and cloudy-clear.

3

When April pours the colours of a shell
Upon the hills, when every little creek
Is shot with silver from the Chesapeake
In shoals new-minted by the ocean swell,
When strawberries go begging, and the sleek
Blue plums lie open to the blackbird's beak,
We shall live well—we shall live very well.

The months between the cherries and the peaches
Are brimming cornucopias which spill
Fruits red and purple, sombre-bloomed and black;
Then, down rich fields and frosty river beaches
We'll trample bright persimmons, while you kill
Bronze partridge, speckled quail, and canvasback.

4

Down to the Puritan marrow of my bones
There's something in this richness that I hate.
I love the look, austere, immaculate,
Of landscapes drawn in pearly monotones.
There's something in my very blood that owns
Bare hills, cold silver on a sky of slate,
A thread of water, churned to milky spate
Streaming through slanted pastures fenced with stone

I love those skies, thin blue or snowy gray,
Those fields sparse-planted, rendering meagre sheave
That spring, briefer than apple-blossom's breath,
Summer, so much too beautiful to stay,
Swift autumn, like a bonfire of leaves,
And sleepy winter, like the sleep of death.

PROPHECY

I shall lie hidden in a hut
   In the middle of an alder wood,
With the back door blind and bolted shut,
   And the front door locked for good.

I shall lie folded like a saint,
   Lapped in a scented linen sheet,
On a bedstead striped with bright-blue paint,
   Narrow and cold and neat.

The midnight will be glassy black
   Behind the panes, with wind about
To set his mouth against a crack
   And blow the candle out.

H. D. (Hilda Doolittle) was born September 10, 1886 in Bethlehem, Pennsylvania. She attended Bryn Mawr, where she met Marianne Moore, but she left because of ill health. In 1911 she went to Europe, where she lived most of her life. In 1913 she married Richard Aldington, whom she later divorced. She began publishing when Ezra Pound sent some of her poems to Harriet Monroe of *Poetry* in 1913, and soon she became known as one of the leaders of the Imagist poets. Her books of poems include *Sea Garden* (1916), *Hymen* (1921), *Heliodora and Other Poems* (1924), *Collected Poems* (1925), *Red Roses from Bronze* (1931), *The Walls Do Not Fall* (1944), *Tribute to the Angels* (1945), and *Collected Poems* (1940). She also wrote novels and did translations from the Greek.

CALLYPSO SPEAKS

Callypso

O you clouds,
here is my song;
man is clumsy and evil
a devil.

O you sand,
this is my command,
drown all men in slow breathless suffocation—
then they may understand.

O you winds,
beat his sails flat,
shift a wave sideways
that he suffocate.

O you waves,
run counter to his oars,
waft him to blistering shores,
where he may die of thirst.

O you skies,
send rain
to wash salt from my eyes,

and witness, all earth and heaven,
it was of my heart-blood
his sails were woven;

witness, river and sea and land;
you, you must hear me—
man is a devil,
man will not understand.

Odysseus (on the sea)

She gave me fresh water in an earth-jar,
strange fruits
to quench thirst,
a golden zither
to work magic on the water;

she gave me wine in a cup
and white wine in a crystal shell;
she gave me water and salt,
wrapped in a palm-leaf,
and palm-dates:

she gave me wool and a pelt of fur,
she gave me a pelt of silver-fox,
and a brown soft skin of a bear,

she gave me an ivory comb for my hair,
she washed brine and mud from my body,
and cool hands
held balm
for a rust-wound;

she gave me water
and fruit in a basket,
and shallow
baskets of pulse and grain, and a ball
of hemp
for mending the sail;

she gave me a willow-basket
for letting into the shallows
for eels;

she gave me peace in her cave.

Callypso (from land)

He has gone,
he has forgotten;
he took my lute and my shell of crystal—
he never looked back—

Odysseus (on the sea)

She gave me a wooden flute
and a mantle,
she wove this wool—

Callypso (from land)

For man is a brute and a fool.

OREAD

Whirl up, sea—
whirl your pointed pines,
splash your great pines
on our rocks,
hurl your green over us,
cover us with your pools of fir.

EVADNE

I first tasted under Apollo's lips,
love and love sweetness,
I, Evadne;
my hair is made of crisp violets
or hyacinth which the wind combs back
across some rock shelf;
I, Evadne,
was mate of the god of light.

His hair was crisp to my mouth,
as the flower of the crocus,
across my cheek,
cool as the silver-cress
on Erotos bank;
between my chin and throat,
his mouth slipped over and over.

Still between my arm and shoulder,
I feel the brush of his hair,
and my hands keep the gold they took,
as they wandered over and over,
that great arm-full of yellow flowers.

From: TRIBUTE TO THE ANGELS

29

We have seen her
the world over,

Our Lady of the Goldfinch,
Our Lady of the Candelabra,

Our Lady of the Pomegranate,
Our Lady of the Chair;

we have seen her, an empress,
magnificent in pomp and grace,

and we have seen her
with a single flower

or a cluster of garden-pinks
in a glass beside her;

we have seen her snood
drawn over her hair,

or her face set in profile
with the blue hood and stars;

we have seen her head bowed down
with the weight of a domed crown,

or we have seen her, a wisp of a girl
trapped in a golden halo;

we have seen her with arrow, with doves
and a heart like a valentine;

we have seen her in fine silks imported
from all over the Levant,

and hung with pearls brought
from the city of Constantine;

we have seen her sleeve
of every imaginable shade

of damask and figured brocade;
it is true,

the painters did very well by her;
it is true, they missed never a line

of the suave turn of the head
or subtle shade of lowered eye-lid

or eye-lids half-raised; you find
her everywhere (or did find),

in cathedral, museum, cloister,
at the turn of the palace stair.

MARIANNE MOORE was born November 15, 1887 near St. Louis, Missouri. She received her B.A. from Bryn Mawr in 1909 and attended Carlisle Commercial College in Pennsylvania in 1910. She first published in *Poetry,* 1915, and went on to publish many books of poems including *Poems* (1921), *Observations* (1924), *Selected Poems* (1935), *What Are Years?* (1941), *Collected Poems* (1951), *Nevertheless* (1956), *Like a Bulwark* (1956), *O To Be a Dragon* (1959), and *Tell Me, Tell Me: Granite, Steel, and Other Topics* (1966). She also wrote plays and essays, and did translations, including the fables of La Fontaine. She was editor of *The Dial* from 1925 to 1929, and she received numerous awards and honors, including the Pulitzer Prize, the National Book Award for Poetry and the Bollingen Prize in poetry for her *Collected Poems.* She died in 1972.

MARRIAGE

This institution,
perhaps one should say enterprise
out of respect for which
one says one need not change one's mind
about a thing one has believed in,
requiring public promises
of one's intention
to fulfil a private obligation:
I wonder what Adam and Eve
think of it by this time,
this fire-gilt steel
alive with goldenness;
how bright it shows—
"of circular traditions and impostures,
committing many spoils,"
requiring all one's criminal ingenuity
to avoid!
Psychology which explains everything
explains nothing,
and we are still in doubt.
Eve: beautiful woman—
I have seen her
when she was so handsome
she gave me a start,
able to write simultaneously
in three languages—
English, German, and French—
and talk in the meantime;
equally positive in demanding a commotion
and in stipulating quiet:
"I should like to be alone";
to which the visitor replies,
"*I* should like to be alone;
why not be alone together?"
Below the incandescent stars
below the incandescent fruit,
the strange experience of beauty;

its existence is too much;
it tears one to pieces
and each fresh wave of consciousness
is poison.
"See her, see her in this common world,"
the central flaw
in that first crystal-fine experiment,
this amalgamation which can never be more
than an interesting impossibility,
describing it
as "that strange paradise
unlike flesh, stones,
gold or stately buildings,
the choicest piece of my life:
the heart rising
in its estate of peace
as a boat rises
with the rising of the water";
constrained in speaking of the serpent—
shed snakeskin in the history of politeness
not to be returned to again—
that invaluable accident
exonerating Adam.
And he has beauty also;
it's distressing—the O thou
to whom from whom,
without whom nothing—Adam;
"something feline,
something colubrine"—how true!
a crouching mythological monster
in that Persian miniature of emerald mines,
raw silk—ivory white, snow white,
oyster white and six others—
that paddock full of leopards and giraffes—
long lemon-yellow bodies
sown with trapezoids of blue.
Alive with words,
vibrating like a cymbal
touched before it has been struck,
he has prophesied correctly—

the industrious waterfall,
"the speedy stream
which violently bears all before it,
at one time silent as the air
and now as powerful as the wind."
"Treading chasms
on the uncertain footing of a spear,"
forgetting that there is in woman
a quality of mind
which as an instinctive manifestation
is unsafe,
he goes on speaking
in a formal customary strain,
of "past states, the present state,
seals, promises,
the evil one suffered,
the good one enjoys,
hell, heaven,
everything convenient
to promote one's joy."
In him a state of mind
perceives what it was not
intended that he should;
"he experiences a solemn joy
in seeing that he has become an idol."
Plagued by the nightingale
in the new leaves,
with its silence—
not its silence but its silences,
he says of it:
"It clothes me with a shirt of fire."
"He dares not clap his hands
to make it go on
lest it fly off;
if he does nothing, it will sleep;
if he cries out, it will not understand."
Unnerved by the nightingale
and dazzled by the apple,
impelled by "the illusion of a fire
effectual to extinguish fire,"

compared with which
the shining of the earth
is but deformity—a fire
"as high as deep
as bright as broad
as long as life itself,"
he stumbles over marriage,
"a very trivial object indeed"
to have destroyed the attitude
in which he stood—
the ease of the philosopher
unfathered by a woman.
Unhelpful Hymen!
a kind of overgrown cupid
reduced to insignificance
by the mechanical advertising
parading as involuntary comment,
by that experiment of Adam's
with ways out but no way in—
the ritual of marriage,
augmenting all its lavishness;
its fiddle-head ferns,
lotus flowers, opuntias, white dromedaries,
its hippopotamus—
nose and mouth combined
in one magnificent hopper—
its snake and the potent apple.
He tells us
that "for love that will
gaze an eagle blind,
that is with Hercules
climbing the trees
in the garden of the Hesperides,
from forty-five to seventy
is the best age,"
commending it
as a fine art, as an experiment,
a duty or as merely recreation.
One must not call him ruffian
nor friction a calamity—

the fight to be affectionate:
"no truth can be fully known
until it has been tried
by the tooth of disputation."
The blue panther with black eyes,
the basalt panther with blue eyes,
entirely graceful—
one must give them the path—
the black obsidian Diana
who "darkeneth her countenance
as a bear doth,"
the spiked hand
that has an affection for one
and proves it to the bone,
impatient to assure you
that impatience is the mark of independence,
not of bondage.
"Married people often look that way"—
"seldom and cold, up and down,
mixed and malarial
with a good day and a bad."
"When do we feed?"
We occidentals are so unemotional,
we quarrel as we feed;
self lost, the irony preserved
in "the Ahasuerus tête-à-tête banquet"
with its small orchids like snakes' tongues,
with its "good monster, lead the way,"
with little laughter
and munificence of humor
in that quixotic atmosphere of frankness
in which, "four o'clock does not exist,
but at five o'clock
the ladies in their imperious humility
are ready to receive you";
in which experience attests
that men have power
and sometimes one is made to feel it.
He says, " 'What monarch would not blush
to have a wife

with hair like a shaving-brush?'
The fact of woman
is 'not the sound of the flute
but very poison.' "
She says, "Men are monopolists
of 'stars, garters, buttons
and other shining baubles'—
unfit to be the guardians
of another person's happiness."
He says, "These mummies
must be handled carefully—
'the crumbs from a lion's meal,
a couple of shins and the bit of an ear';
turn to the letter M
and you will find
that a 'wife is a coffin,'
that severe object
with the pleasing geometry
stipulating space not people,
refusing to be buried
and uniquely disappointing,
revengefully wrought in the attitude
of an adoring child
to a distinguished parent."
She says, "This butterfly,
this waterfly, this nomad
that has 'proposed
to settle on my hand for life.'—
What can one do with it?
There must have been more time
in Shakespeare's day
to sit and watch a play.
You know so many artists who are fools."
He says, "You know so many fools
who are not artists."
The fact forgot
that 'some have merely rights
while some have obligations,'
he loves himself so much,
he can permit himself

no rival in that love.
She loves herself so much,
she cannot see herself enough—
a statuette of ivory on ivory,
the logical last touch
to an expansive splendor
earned as wages for work done:
one is not rich but poor
when one can always seem so right.
What can one do for them—
these savages
condemned to disaffect
all those who are not visionaries
alert to undertake the silly task
of making people noble?
This model of petrine fidelity
who "leaves her peaceful husband
only because she has seen enough of him"—
that orator reminding you,
"I am yours to command."
"Everything to do with love is mystery;
it is more than a day's work
to investigate this science."
One sees that it is rare—
that striking grasp of opposites
opposed each to the other, not to unity,
which in cycloid inclusiveness
has dwarfed the demonstration
of Columbus with the egg—
a triumph of simplicity—
that charitive Euroclydon
of frightening disinterestedness
which the world hates,
admitting:

> "I am such a cow,
> if I had a sorrow
> I should feel it a long time;
> I am not one of those
> who have a great sorrow

in the morning
and a great joy at noon;"

which says: "I have encountered it
among those unpretentious
protégés of wisdom,
where seeming to parade
as the debater and the Roman,
the statesmanship
of an archaic Daniel Webster
persists to their simplicity of temper
as the essence of the matter:

'Liberty and union
now and forever';

the Book on the writing-table;
the hand in the breast-pocket."

EDNA ST. VINCENT MILLAY was born February 22, 1892 in Rockland, Maine. She graduated from Vassar College in 1917, the same year that her first book, *Renascence,* was published. Between then and 1940 she published several volumes of poetry; her *Collected Sonnets* were published in 1941, *Collected Lyrics* in 1943, and *Collected Poems* in 1956 after her death. Her numerous awards include membership in the National Institute of Arts and Letters and the American Academy of Arts and Letters, the Gold Medal of the Poetry Society of America, and the Pulitzer Prize. She recorded her poems for RCA Victor in 1941. She also wrote prose, using the pen name Nancy Boyd. She died on October 19, 1950, and her *Letters* were published in 1952.

27

RENDEZVOUS

Not for these lovely blooms that prank your chambers di
    I come. Indeed,
I could have loved you better in the dark;
That is to say, in rooms less bright with roses, rooms mor
    casual, less aware
Of History in the wings about to enter with benevolent ai
On ponderous tiptoe, at the cue "Proceed."
Not that I like the ash-trays over-crowded and the plac
    in a mess,
Or the monastic cubicle too unctuously austere and stark
But partly that these formal garlands for our Eighth Stree
    Aphrodite are a bit too Greek,
And partly that to make the poor walls rich with our un
    aided loveliness
Would have been more *chic*.

Yet here I am, having told you of my quarrel with th
    taxi-driver over a line of Milton, and you laugh; an
    you are you, none other.
Your laughter pelts my skin with small delicious blows.
But I am perverse: I wish you had not scrubbed—wit
    pumice, I suppose—
The tobacco stains from your beautiful fingers. And I wis
    I did not feel like your mother.

PASSER MORTUUS EST

Death devours all lovely things:
    Lesbia with her sparrow
Shares the darkness,—presently
    Every bed is narrow.

Unremembered as old rain
    Dries the sheer libation;
And the little petulant hand
    Is an annotation.

After all, my erstwhile dear,
My no longer cherished,
Need we say it was not love,
Just because it perished?

JUSTICE DENIED IN MASSACHUSETTS

et us abandon then our gardens and go home
nd sit in the sitting-room.
all the larkspur blossom or the corn grow under this
cloud?
ur to the fruitful seed
the cold earth under this cloud,
stering quack and weed, we have marched upon but
cannot conquer;
e have bent the blades of our hoes against the stalks of
them.

t us go home, and sit in the sitting-room.
ot in our day
all the cloud go over and the sun rise as before,
neficent upon us
it of the glittering bay,
d the warm winds be blown inward from the sea
oving the blades of corn
th a peaceful sound.
rlorn, forlorn,
nds the blue hay-rack by the empty mow.
d the petals drop to the ground,
aving the tree unfruited.
e sun that warmed our stooping backs and withered the
weed uprooted—
shall not feel it again.
shall die in darkness, and be buried in the rain.

at from the splendid dead
have inherited—
rrows sweet to the grain, and the weed subdued—

See now the slug and the mildew plunder.
Evil does overwhelm
The larkspur and the corn;
We have seen them go under.

Let us sit here, sit still,
Here in the sitting-room until we die;
At the step of Death on the walk, rise and go;
Leaving to our children's children this beautiful doorwa
And this elm,
And a blighted earth to till
With a broken hoe.

HUNTSMAN, WHAT QUARRY?

"Huntsman, what quarry
On the dry hill
Do your hounds harry?

When the red oak is bare
And the white oak still
Rattles its leaves
In the cold air:
What fox runs there?"

"Girl, gathering acorns
In the cold autumn,
I hunt the hot pads
That ever run before,
I hunt the pointed mask
That makes no reply,
I hunt the red brush
Of remembered joy."

"To tame or to destroy?"

"To destroy."

"Huntsman, hard by
In a wood of grey beeches
Whose leaves are on the ground,
Is a house with a fire;
You can see the smoke from here.
There's supper and a soft bed
And not a soul around.
Come with me there;
Bide there with me;
And let the fox run free."

The horse that he rode on
Reached down its neck,
Blew upon the acorns,
Nuzzled them aside;
The sun was near setting;
He thought, "Shall I heed her?"
He thought, "Shall I take her
For a one-night's bride?"

He smelled the sweet smoke,
He looked the lady over;
Her hand was on his knee;
But like a flame from cover
The red fox broke—
And "Hoick! Hoick!" cried he.

Sam Tamashira

BABETTE DEUTSCH was born in New York City in 1895. She received her B.A. from Barnard College, and her poems began appearing in periodicals while she was an undergraduate there. Her first book, *Banners,* was published in 1919. Since then she has published nine other books of poems. She is also the author of juvenile books, fiction, and criticism including *Poetry in Our Time* and *The Poetry Handbook.* With her husband, Avrahm Yarmolinsky, she has made many translations from the Russian poets, including Pushkin's *Eugene Onegin;* among her other translations is *Poems from the Book of Hours* by Rilke. From 1944 to 1971 she gave a course in twentieth century poetry at Columbia University, and that university awarded her an honorary Litt. D. She is a member of the National Institute of Arts and Letters and served as its secretary from 1969 through 1971.

NATURAL LAW

If you press a stone with your finger,
Sir Isaac Newton observed,
The finger is also
Pressed by the stone.
But can a woman, pressed by memory's finger,
In the deep night, alone,
Of her softness move
The airy thing
That presses upon her
With the whole weight of love? This
Sir Isaac said nothing of.

THE MOTHER

On the hilltop, close to the house of the empress,
    Your temple
Is dark, sunken: a pit. The thick crowded pillars
Stumps only. The dread of Your presence
Stopped, like them, cold in mutilation.
Throning it here, in the stillness: vacancy.
In times beyond this time, were you robed in darkness?
You were known, then, as the Great Goddess. You are
Great even yet, more terrible, Mother Cybele, now you
    are nothing.

LOUISE BOGAN was born in 1897 in Livermore Falls, Maine. Her books include *Body of This Death* (1923), *Dark Summer* (1929), *The Sleeping Fury* (1937), *Poems and New Poems* (1941), and most recently *The Blue Estuaries*. She won numerous awards from *Poetry* magazine, and her *Collected Poems, 1923–1953* won the Bollingen Prize in Poetry, 1954. She contributed a volume on the history of American poetry from 1900 to 1950 to the *Twentieth-Century Literature in America* series, and she became known for her poetry criticism written for *The New Yorker* Magazine.

MEDUSA

I had come to the house, in a cave of trees,
Facing a sheer sky.
Everything moved,—a bell hung ready to strike,
Sun and reflection wheeled by.

When the bare eyes were before me
And the hissing hair,
Held up at a window, seen through a door.
The stiff bald eyes, the serpents on the forehead
Formed in the air.

This is a dead scene forever now.
Nothing will ever stir.
The end will never brighten it more than this,
Nor the rain blur.

The water will always fall, and will not fall,
And the tipped bell make no sound.
The grass will always be growing for hay
Deep on the ground.

And I shall stand here like a shadow
Under the great balanced day,
My eyes on the yellow dust, that was lifting in the wind,
And does not drift away.

CASSANDRA

To me, one silly task is like another.
I bare the shambling tricks of lust and pride.
This flesh will never give a child its mother,—
Song, like a wing, tears through my breast, my side,
And madness chooses out my voice again,
Again. I am the chosen no hand saves:
The shrieking heaven lifted over men,
Not the dumb earth, wherein they set their graves.

THE SLEEPING FURY

You are here now,
Who were so loud and feared, in a symbol before me,
Alone and asleep, and I at last look long upon you.

Your hair fallen on your cheek, no longer in the semblanc
    of serpents,
Lifted in the gale; your mouth, that shrieked so, silent.
You, my scourge, my sister, lie asleep, like a child,
Who, after rage, for an hour quiet, sleeps out its tears.

The days close to winter
Rough with strong sound. We hear the sea and the fores
And the flames of your torches fly, lit by others,
Ripped by the wind, in the night. The black sheep fo
    sacrifice
Huddle together. The milk is cold in the jars.

All to no purpose, as before, the knife whetted ar
    plunged,
The shout raised, to match the clamor you have give
    them.
You alone turn away, not appeased; unaltered, avenger.

Hands full of scourges, wreathed with your flames an
    adders,
You alone turned away, but did not move from my sid
Under the broken light, when the soft nights took th
    torches.

At thin morning you showed, thick and wrong in that calr
The ignoble dream and the mask, sly, with slits at the eye
Pretence and half-sorrow, beneath which a coward's hop
    trembled.

You uncovered at night, in the locked stillness of house
False love due the child's heart, the kissed-out lie, th
    embraces,

ade by the two who for peace tenderly turned to each
other.

ou who know what we love, but drive us to know it;
ou with your whips and shrieks, bearer of truth and of
solitude;
ou who give, unlike men, to expiation your mercy.

opping the scourge when at last the scourged advances
to meet it,
u, when the hunted turns, no longer remain the hunter
t stand silent and wait, at last returning his gaze.

autiful now as a child whose hair, wet with rage and
tears,
ngs to its face. And now I may look upon you,
ving once met your eyes. You lie in sleep and forget me.
one and strong in my peace, I look upon you in yours.

LORINE NIEDECKER was born on May 12, 1903
near Fort Atkinson, Wisconsin. She spent most of
her life in this area near the mouth of the Rock River
where it enters Lake Koshkonong. She studied
at Beloit College and worked for the radio station at the University of Wisconsin at Madison.
She was an assistant in a local library and then
"when eyes went a bit bad" worked in hospitals and
dining rooms "washing floors, etc." She avoided the
public poetry scene, but did have several close friendships with poets, in particular Louis Zukofsky, who
included her in his *Objectivist Anthology*. In 196
she married Albert Millen, and traveled widely with
him; for her it was almost the first time she ventured
out of her native area, but they continued to live on
Blackhawk Island where she grew up. Her books of
poems include *T & G* (Tenderness and Gristle),
Jargon Books, and *North Central* and *My Life by
Water, Collected Poems 1936–1968*, Fulcrum Press.
She died on December 31, 1970.

Old Mother turns blue and from us,
   "Don't let my head drop to the earth.
I'm blind and deaf."   Death from the heart,
   a thimble in her purse.

"It's a long day since last night.
   Give me space.   I need
floors.   Wash the floors, Lorine!—
   wash clothes!   Weed!"

*

     River-marsh-drowse
     and in flood
         moonlight
            gives sight
  of no land.

     They fish, a man
     takes his wife to town
     with his rowboat's 10-horse
        ships his voice
     to the herons.

     Sure they drink
     —full foamy folk—
         till asleep.
     The place is asleep
  on one leg in the weeds.

*

In the great snowfall before the bomb
colored yule tree lights
windows, the only glow for contemplation
along this road

I worked the print shop
right down among em
the folk from whom all poetry flows
and dreadfully much else.

I was Blondie
I carried my bundles of hog feeder price lists
down by Larry the Lug,
I'd never get anywhere

because I'd never had suction,
pull, you know, favor, drag,
well-oiled protection.

I heard their rehashed radio barbs—
more barbarous among hirelings
as higher-ups grow more corrupt.
But what vitality!   The women hold jobs—
clean house, cook, raise children, bowl
and go to church.

What would they say if they knew
I sit for two months on six lines
of poetry?

PAEAN TO PLACE

*And the place
was water*

Fish
      fowl
           flood
        Water lily mud
My life

in the leaves and on water
My mother and I
              born
in swale and swamp and sworn
to water

My father

thru marsh fog
    sculled down
        from high ground
saw her face

at the organ
bore the weight of lake water
    and the cold—
he seined for carp to be sold
that their daughter

might go high
on land
    to learn
Saw his wife turn
deaf

and away
She
    who knew boats
        and ropes
no longer played

She helped him string out nets
for tarring
    And she could shoot
        He was cool
to the man

who stole his minnows
by night and next day offered
    to sell them back
        He brought in a sack
of dandelion greens

if no flood
No oranges—none at hand
    No marsh marigolds
        where the water rose
He kept us afloat

I mourn her not hearing canvasbacks
their blast-off rise
    from the water
        Not hearing sora
rail's sweet

spoon-tapped waterglass-
descending scale-
    tear-drop-tittle
        Did she giggle
as a girl?

His skiff skimmed
the coiled celery now gone
    from these streams
        due to carp
He knew duckweed

fall-migrates
toward Mud Lake bottom
    Knew what lay
        under leaf decay
and on pickerelweeds

before summer hum
To be counted on:
    new leaves
        new dead
leaves

He could not
—like water bugs—
    stride surface tension
        He netted
loneliness

As to his bright new car
my mother—her house
    next his—averred:
        A hummingbird
can't haul

Anchored here
in the rise and sink
    of life—
        middle years' nights
he sat

beside his shoes
rocking his chair
    Roped not 'looped
        in the loop
of her hair'

I grew in green
slide and slant
    of shore and shade
        Child-time—wade
thru weeds

Maples to swing from
Pewee-glissando
    sublime
        slime-
song

Grew riding the river
Books
    at home-pier
        Shelley could steer
as he read

I was the solitary plover
a pencil
    for a wing-bone

From the secret notes
I must tilt

upon the pressure
execute and adjust
    In us sea-air rhythm
'We live by the urgent wave
of the verse'

Seven-year molt
for the solitary bird
    and so young
Seven years the one
dress

for town once a week
One for home
    faded blue-striped
as she piped
her cry

Dancing grounds
my people had none
    woodcocks had—
    backland-
air around

Solemnities
such as what flower
    to take
    to grandfather's grave
unless

water lilies—
he who'd bowed his head
    to grass as he mowed
    Iris now grows
on fill

for the two
and for him
       where they lie
       How much less am I
in the dark than they?

Effort lay in us
before religions
       at pond bottom
              All things move toward
the light

except those
that freely work down
       to oceans' black depths
              In us an impulse tests
the unknown

River rising—flood
Now melt and leave home
       Return—broom wet
              naturally wet
Under

soak-heavy rug
water bugs hatched—
       no snake in the house
              Where were they?—
she

who knew how to clean up
after floods
       he who bailed boats, houses
              Water endows us
with buckled floors

You with sea water running
in your veins sit down in water
    Expect the long-stemmed blue
        speedwell to renew

itself

O my floating life
Do not save love
    for things
        Throw *things*

to the flood

ruined
by the flood
    Leave the new unbought—
        all one in the end—

water

I possessed
the high word:
    The boy my friend
        played his violin

in the great hall

On this stream
my moonnight memory
    washed of hardships
        maneuvers barges

thru the mouth

of the river
They fished in beauty
    It was not always so
        In Fishes

red Mars

rising
rides the sloughs and sluices
    of my mind
        with the persons

on the edge

Kenneth S. Lane

KAY BOYLE, a native of St. Paul, Minnesota, has lived much of her life in France, Austria, England and Germany. She is now Professor of English at San Francisco State College. The author of more than twenty books, including short stories, novels, children's books and poetry, she is a member of the National Institute of Arts and Letters and the recipient of two Guggenheim Fellowships and two O. Henry awards for her short stories. Among her most recent works are *Being Geniuses Together, Nothing Ever Breaks Except the Heart* and *Generation Without Farewell*. Her *Collected Poems* was published by Alfred A. Knopf and *Testament for My Students* by Doubleday.

47

FOR MARIANNE MOORE'S BIRTHDAY

November 15, 1967

I wish you triumphs that are yours already,
And also wish to say whatever I have done
Has been in admiration (imitation even)
Of all you marvelously proliferate. Once someone
Turned to me and said in lowered voice (because you too
    were in the room)
That William Carlos Williams gave to you at sight that
Singular esteem known by no other name save love. These
    words were
Spoken perhaps a half century ago
(In Monroe Wheeler's Eastside flat) when you
Wore amber braids around your head. And now,
As then, I cannot write this book or that
Without you. You have always been
Nightingale, baseball fan, librarian of my visions,
Poised on a moving ladder in the sun.

From: **AMERICAN CITIZEN**

The Invitation in It

Carson, turn your coat collar up, throw the cigarette from
    your hand
And dance with me. The mazurka of women is easy to
    learn.
It is danced by the young, the high-heeled, and the doll
    faced
Who swing on the bar stools, their soft drinks before
    them.
The polka of war brides is easy to follow. They dance
    down the streets

With their legs bare, their coats hanging open. In their
     pockets
Are letters written from home to be opened
Not to be read, but ripped wide by the fingernail
     (varnished
The color of blood), to be shaken for the check or the
     money order,
The dollar bill folded. These are the honeymooners
In one-room shacks, in overnight cabins, in trailer camps,
     dancing
The *pas seul* in shoes that strap fast at the ankle, talking
G.I. talk as if they had learned it not this year,
Not here, but months at the breast, years learning to spell
     still.
"Sweating out three weeks of maneuvers, or sweating the
     week-end pass,
Or sweating him out night after night," they'll say,
     sweet-tongued as thrushes.
"Say, who's fighting this war, the M.P.'s or our husbands?"
     they'll ask
As they swing on the bar stools. Their voices may say:
"Up on Kiska last year, he lost eighty bucks in a crap
     game
And twelve playing cards, two weeks before Christmas,"
While the music plays on for the dancers; or say:
"This is my ring. How do you like it? We didn't have
     diamonds
Put in this year. We can get them cheaper back home.
We were going to have something engraved inside. We
     wanted 'forever'
Engraved, but we didn't have time yet," or saying:
"The night I had fever he wanted to go over the hill,"
But where is the hill that is high enough, wild enough, lost
     enough
Leading away? (Carson, dance with me.) This is the waltz
Of the wives whose men are in khaki. Their faces are
     painted
As flawless as children's, their hearts each the flame of a
     candle
That his breath can extinguish at will.

OCTOBER 1954

Now the time of year has come for the leaves to be
    burning.
October, and the month fills me with grief
For the girl who used to run with the black dogs through
    them,
Singing, before they burned. Light as a leaf
Her heart, and her mouth red as the sumac turning.

Oh, girl, come back to tell them with your bell-like singing
That you are this figure who stands alone, watching the
    dead leaves burn.
(The wind is high in the trees, and the clang of bluejay
    voices ringing
Turns the air to metal. This is not a month for anyone who
    grieves.)
For they would say that a witch had passed in fury if I
    should turn,
Gray-haired and brooding, and run now as I once ran
    through the leaves.

William Wachtel

HELEN WOLFERT was born in New York City. She received her B.A. from Hunter College, and was a teacher in the New York City schools for ten years. She was the poetry reviewer for the newspaper *PM*, and she has had poems, short stories, articles and reviews published in various magazines, newspapers and anthologies. Her books of poetry are *Nothing Is a Wonderful Thing*, Simon and Schuster, 1946, and *The Music*, W. W. Norton, 1965. She has been occupied for some years in a study of a new interpretation of "The Song of Songs." She is married and has a daughter and a son. She has traveled extensively over the world with her husband.

THE CAT

The leaves hang like fruit in your eyes, autumn cat.
Art is a dream and I choose to dream you.
Lo you! flowery-lipped, a sculpture of all cats.
I have known them always with an old knowing.
But you, you are new and impossible and the one and the
　　cat before cats,
And my dream is my dream before and after.

Lo you! And lustrous you come, earth-brown, sea-dipped,
　　you
Cat out of old rooms, out of gardens in a rush, together,
You, cat I had forgotten and you, cat of cats,
Incorporeal out of the sky pure as out of a wood,
Pluming your haunches, all, until you are hummocks in
　　the sun;
And wooling closer, cloudier,
Lunar gray fur on lunar gray fur,
Thistle bloom in bloom on thistle bloom in bloom,
And finally grass, a heather of cats.

Lo you!—It is moon time. It is sun time.—Long over out
　　of the gauze
Distance I have called; and out of matted foliages,
Out of time and times you have come,
And where no cat sat, on the horizon
Where no horizon was, you sit, autumn cat,
Your mane of manes smoothed down
Like a single, solid triangle, illumined and never to die;
—It is dream time. It is stone time.—
Your pomegranate breasts entombed;
The papayas in your eyes closed over;
—It is new time. It is one time.—
The orbs of night and day on your sanded green paws.

So I have dreamed you, woman cat woman,
Flowery-lipped, stonily-hipped, great she
Chipped out of stone.

o I have dreamed you, woman cat woman, glooming or
    golding: forever you
nd forever my own.
o I have dreamed you and invented Egypt.

From: WOMAN AGAINST THE MOON

The preparation of the body

tand mute in the moonshine and lights of the moon
at go over my body are fingers that change
ce again what I am, a warm statue of woman
at stood steadfast already, supreme and complete.

tood slim and myself in the moon, but the fingers
ve added warm clay to my limbs and have made
em like brown earthen jars and as if they were flooded
th milk and with honey and gold oil of palm.
y two breasts that were fine and as white as are
        mushrooms
e now covered with honey, and fingers of moon
ve rounded them as with the pulp of a fruit.
This is honey, milk and yellow broom of rye,
It is bush and pomegranate, but not I.
It is Venus and her blossom flesh upon
My immaculately sculpted skeleton.
It is Mother Ceres plowing wider lanes
Through my needle-narrow and pin-pointed veins.
It is apples cumulus upon the tree,
It is earth and grass the moon has made of me.

Where the mind meets the moon in revolt

a sudden and sharp I arise from the loam
the moonlight and point my gray arm at the moon;
Moon, globed and glamorous moon,
Moon, willful and terrible moon,
ift your lean and fleshy fingers from me, Moon.

Moon, salt and ocean-harsh moon,
Moon, falling and down-weeping moon,
Strike from off my face, the tears, the little moons.

Moon, bloomed and full-bodied moon,
Moon, whirling-in-ecstasy-moon,
Cut me from the rhythm of your fullness, Moon.

Cursed white be your white, O Moon.
Doom come to you in your bloom,
Cursèd be the flower of the universe.

Moon I am not, and flower not;
Broke, blended am I to them both.
Flower and fingers, rhythm, Moonlight, let me be!

And the pour of the moonlight swims over my body.

THE GRASS

When you begin, begin at the beginning.
Marble! Marble awash!
Out of the center the sun
Is a sea of waves ahoying, hallooing
With smoky vowels, with a smash of brasses.
The sky is falling in milk, chiffoning under
With a coiffure of tulips, with a
Cave of cherries; ships of fish fly through the ferner
    sprigs of sand
Spring up, bouquets of clay, and finally, he,
Wine, purple and masculine, triumphant,
A man with obsidian eyes
Carrying green in his hands, a lake of moss.

When you begin, begin at the beginning.
Marble: the cascade of crescents, the choir of wine m
The floss of slipperinesses and Fire.
Over it and under and in it, Fire,

Till it shoots and tassels, till it crouches and crowds, till
    it flowers and fogs,
Till it spills and is flat and is glass
And a street and smooth, so we may walk on it with our
    feet.

When you begin, begin at the beginning.
Begin with magic, begin with the sun,
Begin with the grass.

Sydney Rachel Goldstein

ROSALIE MOORE was born October 8, 1910 in
Oakland, California. She received her B.A. with
highest honors in English from the University of
California at Berkeley, and her M.A. Phi Beta Kappa
in English. She feels that her main learning experience was with Lawrence Hart, whose class organized
the Activist group of poets. This class led to her
publication of *The Grasshopper's Man and Other
Poems* in the Yale Younger Poets Series, 1949. The
recipient of two Guggenheim Fellowships, she also
had twelve years of piano study and is a member of
the California Music Teachers' Association. She had
a short career as a radio writer and announcer. She
married in 1942 and has three daughters. With her
husband, Bill Brown, she wrote ten children's books.
Her husband died in 1964, and she is now teaching
at the College of Marin in the Communications
Department. In the fall of 1972 she had a sabbatical
leave and planned to work on a book of poetry.

IMPRECATION FOR AN
AESTHETICS SOCIETY
WITH NEWTS, WARTS,
WAXES AND PINS

m ready now to cat-chase those porcelain people, get
   after them
ith bells like fire buckets, damn them
ith my own personal damn.

t them float into the gardens like little images
  saint formation.
will spank their loaves
ith a butterfly spanker.

ither shall I retreat,
 lemon light and at tea-tile,
e narrow man, half cloak,
sage of hornet—
w he lifts with his tongs a lid,
lf open Dante,
lows, briefly, the tongues to chime
ke cricket box.

hieve, if you will, in the room—
 brilliant suffocation of cat fight—
speech, as of mouse to mouse
 antenna flicker,
 needle-whisk.

t them wear taller hats to show who they are;
burnt beetle like an imitation butler
averses their underwear.

e goldfish leap in their vases.
   The gullet grate
ens its plaza of dark.

THE WHEEL

The sea laying it down, the sea saying it,
In the ear's wheel, casino of self,
The sea saying it.

Near my face is a horneted
Constellation of faces;
In my blood,
A wire to win.

The sea saying it, with cast ships,
With gambler's matches.

Girl, goddess in a hip's narrows,
That wishing machine you pray by
Is no boy-bringer.
O mouth with a crestfall of pennies;
My true heart lies within
A nickel-fall of this.

Out on the sea is a truer rising
Of wires without ships.
The stars cross in the life lines, and the sea
Saying, saying it, under.

One at the thin edge bends, and the hair floats forwar
Rise, as to try no more
The neck's stem of coral.

    O daughter,
Pull from the water and see crumple
The pimpled star. Comfort your cold with cold.
And the reef of the rocky stars seems to your ship
Far over and far out,
As in a dream about that other woman
The mariners beware of.

AFTER THE STORM

Along the streaming ground, the wet leaves fit like fish
And shine like talk.
The prints of the xylophone horses
Clang and revise
Their clear and candid marks.

And only a funeral under a tall quartz sky
Can bring us together as steeply
As these oak trees
And this tomb.

All talk seems genuine: the syllables make evident
Their wild, pronounced colonies.

The word is out—a racket of hail and rhyme
Or landing a few Greek letters at a time.

If any have other knowledge of the crime,
Let him speak, lest the privilege harden;
Let us acknowledge
The rains were heavy and the damage severe—

But there are times when the uncut universe comes close
And whets like a diamond,
And the useful joy seems near.

And the diamond is odd in its meaning,
It rests like a water-mark,
Or read by the shining door.

Christa Fleischmann

JOSEPHINE MILES was born in 1911 in Illinois.
She is now living in Berkeley and has been teaching
at the University of California at Berkeley since
1940. Her books of poems include *Poems 1930–1960*
and *Kinds of Affection* (1967). Her work has appeared in *Poet's Choice* and other anthologies, and
she was one of the California poets to be recorded
on *Today's Poets II*. She has received the National
Institute of the Arts Award and the Blumenthal
Award from *Poetry*, and her criticism has been published in several volumes.

RIDE

It's not my world, I grant, but I made it.
It's not my ranch, lean oak, buzzard crow,
Not my fryers, mixmaster, well-garden.
And now it's down the road and I made it.

It's not your rackety car but you drive it.
It's not your four-door, top-speed, white-wall tires,
Not our state, not even, I guess, our nation,
But now it's down the road, and we're in it.

MAXIM

is said that ceratin orientational concepts of an onto-
   logical sort
h as despair, sin, salvation, loneliness
rive a certain richness from experience.

oticed today at the Rose Bowl Parade
the Romeo and Juliet float representing Wonder Bread,
w lonely Romeo shirtsleeved

the frosty morning air looked, saluting
the balcony made of thousands of blossoms of pink
   winter stock,
d (2) the curbstone crowd.

s won the sweepstakes prize, yet Juliet
led in despair in the frosty morning air,
eiving her certain richness from experience.

HOUSEWIFE

Occasional mornings when an early fog
Not yet dispersed stands in every yard
And drips and undiscloses, she is severely
Put to the task of herself.

Usually here we have view window dawns,
The whole East Bay at least some spaces into the roo
Puffing the curtains, and then she is out
In the submetropolitan stir.

But when the fog at the glass pauses and closes
She is put to ponder
A life-line, how it chooses to run obscurely
In her hand, before her.

MIDWEEK

Plentiful people went to the Cadillac drawing,
My ticket was number nine seven two seven one,
And my friend's ticket was number nine seven two se
    two,
Certainly a lucky number and easy to remember.
I thought of it all through the film, and I like Greer Gar

O heaven when the lights went up, the table trundled
The number called didn't even begin with a nine.
There wasn't even that much respite of hope after
    happy ending.
That is the kind of change the brave buckle
Time and again to.

All those people heart-rent and rustling,
I wished the upper lights would not look down so,
The curtain not so aquamarine, the manager not in tux
Me not so pale. I wished the second feature
Dark and dreadful.

PLAYERS

o the spacious bay the sun of afternoon
one,
d there two people, a man with a beard and a woman
 without, were playing
cards alone.

e traffic, line traffic, pine, plain traffic all around them
sided,
red but soft, rushed but not
o the window many-sided,

oking for a game to play, a war to win, some sort of
 magnificent errand
be done;
ile the spadebeard took easily a trick
eady a century won.

MAY SARTON was born in Wondelgem, Belgium,
May 3, 1911. She came to the U.S. in 1916 and was
naturalized in Boston in 1924. She now divides her
year between Cambridge, Massachusetts, and Nelson,
New Hampshire. She did not go to college but was an
apprentice at Eva Le Gallienne's Civic Repertory Theatre in New York in 1930. Later she was the founder
and director of the Apprentice Theatre. She has
lectured on poetry, has taught creative writing,
and has been a script writer for documentary
films. Her awards include a large grant from the
National Foundation on the Arts and the Humanities.
She has written twelve novels, two autobiographies,
and eleven books of poetry, the latest of which are
A Grain of Mustard Seed and *A Durable Fire*, both
published by W. W. Norton.

From: THE INVOCATION TO KALI

". . . the Black Goddess Kali, the terrible one of
many names, 'difficult of approach,' whose stomach is a void and so can never be filled, and whose
womb is giving birth forever to all things . . ."
Joseph Campbell, *The Masks of God: Oriental Mythology*, The Viking Press, Inc. 1962, p. 5.

I

There are times when
I think only of killing
The voracious animal
Who is my perpetual shame,

The violent one
Whose raging demands
Break down peace and shelter
Like a peacock's scream.

There are times when
I think only of how to do away
With this brute power
That cannot be tamed.

I am the cage where poetry
Paces and roars. The beast
Is the god. How murder the god?
How live with the terrible god?

2

The Kingdom of Kali

Anguish is always there, lurking at night,
Wakes us like a scourge, the creeping sweat
As rage is remembered, self-inflicted blight.
What is it in us we have not mastered yet?

What Hell have we made of the subtle weaving
Of nerve with brain, that all centers tear?
We live in a dark complex of rage and grieving.
The machine grates, grates, whatever we are.

The kingdom of Kali is within us deep.
The built-in destroyer, the savage goddess,
Wakes in the dark and takes away our sleep.
She moves through the blood to poison gentleness.

She keeps us from being what we long to be;
Tenderness withers under her iron laws.
We may hold her like a lunatic, but it is she
Held down, who bloodies with her claws.

How then to set her free or come to terms
With the volcano itself, the fierce power
Erupting injuries, shrieking alarms?
Kali among her skulls must have her hour.

It is time for the invocation, to atone
For what we fear most and have not dared to face:
Kali, the destroyer, cannot be overthrown;
We must stay, open-eyed, in the terrible place.

Every creation is born out of the dark.
Every birth is bloody. Something gets torn.
Kali is there to do her sovereign work
Or else the living child will be still-born.

She cannot be cast out (she is here for good)
Nor battled to the end. Who wins that war?
She cannot be forgotten, jailed, or killed.
Heaven must still be balanced against her.

Out of destruction she comes to wrest
The juice from the cactus, its harsh spine,
And until she, the destroyer, has been blest,
There will be no child, no flower, and no wine.

*　　*　　*

5

It is time for the invocation:

Kali, be with us.
Violence, destruction, receive our homage.
Help us to bring darkness into the light,
To lift out the pain, the anger,
Where it can be seen for what it is—
The balance-wheel for our vulnerable, aching love.
Put the wild hunger where it belongs,
Within the act of creation,
Crude power that forges a balance
Between hate and love.

Help us to be the always hopeful
Gardeners of the spirit
Who know that without darkness
Nothing comes to birth
As without light
Nothing flowers.

Bear the roots in mind,
You, the dark one, Kali,
Awesome power.

MURIEL RUKEYSER was born December 15, 1913 in New York City. She is a graduate of Vassar College and Columbia University, and she has taught at Sarah Lawrence College. She is the author of ten volumes of poetry, four books of prose, several children's books, and translations of Octavio Paz and Gunnar Ekelof. Her own works have been translated into many languages. She holds the Swedish Academy Translation Award and many of America's top prizes for poetry, among them a Guggenheim Fellowship and a grant from the National Foundation on the Arts. She is a member of the National Institute of Arts and Letters, the Society of American Historians, and the History of Science Society. Her latest volumes of poetry are *The Speed of Darkness* and *Waterlily Fire*.

THE POEM AS MASK

ORPHEUS

When I wrote of the women in their dances and wildness,
    it was a mask,
on their mountain, god-hunting, singing, in orgy,
it was a mask; when I wrote of the god,
fragmented, exiled from himself, his life, the love gone
    down with song,
it was myself, split open, unable to speak, in exile from
    myself.

There is no mountain, there is no god, there is memory
of my torn life, myself split open in sleep, the rescued child
beside me among the doctors, and a word
of rescue from the great eyes.

No more masks! No more mythologies!

Now, for the first time, the god lifts his hand,
the fragments join in me with their own music.

A LITTLE STONE IN
THE MIDDLE OF THE ROAD,
IN FLORIDA

My son as a child saying
God
    anything, even a little stone in the middle of the road,
    in Florida.
Yesterday
Nancy, my friend, after long illness:
    You know what can lift me up, take me right out of
    despair?
No, what?
Anything.

KATHE KOLLWITZ

I

Held between wars
my lifetime
                among wars, the big hands of the world of death
my lifetime
listens to yours.

The faces of the sufferers
in the street, in dailiness,
their lives showing
through their bodies
a look as of music
the revolutionary look
that says   I am in the world
to change the world
my lifetime
is to love to endure to suffer the music
to set its portrait
up as a sheet of the world
the most moving the most alive
Easter and bone
and Faust walking among the flowers of the world
and the child alive within the living woman, music of man
and death holding my lifetime between great hands
the hands of enduring life
that suffers the gifts and madness of full life, on earth,
        our time,
and through my life, through my eyes, through my arm
        and hands
may give the face of this music in portrait waiting for
the unknown person
held in the two hands, you.

II

Woman as gates, saying:
"The process is after all like music,
like the development of a piece of music.
The fugues come back and

again and again
interweave.
A theme may seem to have been put aside,
but it keeps returning—
the same thing modulated,
somewhat changed in form.
Usually richer.
And it is very good that this is so."

A woman pouring her opposites.
"After all there are happy things in life too.
Why do you show only the dark side?"
"I could not answer this. But I know—
in the beginning my impulse to know
the working life
had little to do with
pity or sympathy.
I simply felt
that the life of the workers was beautiful."

She said, "I am groping in the dark."

She said, "When the door opens, of sensuality,
then you will understand it too. The struggle begins.
Never again to be free of it,
often you will feel it to be your enemy.
Sometimes
you will almost suffocate,
such joy it brings."

Saying of her husband: "My wish
is to die after Karl.

I know no person who can love as he can,
with his whole soul.
Often this love has oppressed me;
I wanted to be free.
But often too it has made me
so terribly happy."

She said: "We rowed over to Carrara at dawn,
climbed up to the marble quarries
and rowed back at night. The drops of water
fell like glittering stars
from our oars."

She said: "As a matter of fact,
I believe
       that bisexuality
is almost   a necessary factor
in artistic production; at any rate,
the tinge of masculinity within me
helped me
       in my work."

She said: "The only technique I can still manage.
It's hardly a technique at all, lithography.
In it
    only the essentials count."

A tight-lipped man in a restaurant last night
      saying to me:
"Kollwitz?   She's too black-and-white."

III

Held among wars, watching
   all of them
   all these people
   weavers,
   Carmagnole

Looking at
  all of them
  death, the children
  patients in waiting-rooms
  famine
  the street
  the corpse with the baby
  floating, on the dark river

A woman seeing
  the violent, inexorable
  movement of nakedness
  and the confession of No
  the confession of great weakness, war,
  all streaming to one son killed, Peter;
  even the son left living; repeated
  the father, the mother; the grandson
  another Peter killed in another war; firestorm;
  dark, light, as two hands,
  this pole and that pole as the gates.

What would happen if one woman told the truth about
    her life?
  The world would split open

IV

SONG: THE CALLING-UP

Rumor, stir of ripeness
rising within this girl
sensual blossoming
of meaning, its light and form.

The birth-cry summoning
out of the male, the father
from the warm woman
mother in response.

The word of death
calls up the fight with stone
wrestle with grief with time
from the material make
an art harder than bronze.

V

SELF-PORTRAIT

Mouth looking directly at you
eyes in their inwardness looking
directly at you
half light   half darkness
woman, strong, German, young artist
flows into
wide sensual mouth meditating
looking right at you
eyes shadowed with brave hand
looking deep at you
flows into
wounded brave mouth
grieving and hooded eyes
alive, German, in her first War
flows into
strength of the worn face
a skein of lines
broods, flows into
mothers among the war graves
bent over death
facing the father
stubborn upon the field
flows into
the marks of her knowing—
Nie Wieder Krieg
repeated in the eyes
flows into
"Seedcorn must not be ground"
and the grooved cheek
lips drawn fine
the down-drawn grief

face of our age
flows into
Pieta, mother and
between her knees
life as her son in death
pouring from the sky of
one more war
flows into
face almost obliterated
hand over the mouth forever
hand over one eye now
the other great eye
closed

BARBARA HOWES was born in 1914 in New York City. She now makes her home in North Pownal, Vermont, and is a frequent visitor to the West Indies. A graduate of Bennington College, her honors include a Guggenheim Fellowship, a Brandeis University Creative Arts Poetry Grant, and an award in literature from the National Institute of Arts and Letters. Her books of poems include *The Undersea Farmer, In the Cold Country, Light and Dark, Looking Up at Leaves,* and *The Blue Garden.* She is also the editor of *Twenty-three Modern Short Stories, From the Green Antilles,* and *The Eye of the Heart: Short Stories from Latin America.*

DANAË

Golden, within this golden hive
Wild bees drone,
As if at any moment they may
Swarm and be gone
From the arched fibres of their cage,
Lithe as whalebone.

Over a pasture, once, I saw
A flock of small
Martins flying in concert, high
Then wheeling, fall;
Like buckshot pent in a string bag
They dotted all

That sky-patch, holding form in their flight,
A vase poured,
Their breathing shape hung in the air—
Below, the road
Fled secretly as quicksilver:
My eyes blurred.

All things come to their pinnacle
Though landscapes shift,
Women sit in the balance, as
Upon a knife;
Irony cuts to the quick—is this
Life or new life?

They sit their years out on a scale,
The heavy yoke
Of their heavy stomachs grounding them—
Or else come back
To barrenness with each full moon;
Minds go slack

Longing, or dreading, that a new
Form will take shape.

(The martins' swarming is a brush-stroke
On the landscape,
Within their white-gold, fleshly hall
The wild bees wake.)

Homing at close of day, they meet
This moment: now:
Love calls from its subterranean passage,
The bed they know
May support agony or joy—
To bed they go.

LIGHT AND DARK

Lady, take care; for in the diamond eyes
Of old old men is figured your undoing;
Love is turned in behind the wrinkled lids
To nurse their fear and scorn at their near going.
Flesh hangs like the curtains in a house
Long unused, damp as cellars without wine;
They are the future of us all, when we
Will be dried-leaf-thin, the sour whine
Of a siren's diminuendo. They have no past
But egg-husks shattered to a rubbish heap
By memory's looting. Do not follow them
To their camp pitched in a cranny, do not keep
To the road for them, a weary weary yard
Will bring you in; that beckoning host ahead,
Inn-keeper Death, has but to lift his hat
To topple the oldster in the dust. Read,
Poor old man, the sensual moral; sleep
Narrow in your bed, wear no
More so bright a rose in your lapel;
The spell of the world is loosed, it is time to go.

BARBARA HOWES · 79

THE NEW LEDA

oosegirl, your feet are slow
nd heavy with acceptance, while the echo
f what will come
athers momentum and batters at your eardrum.

e future hangs
ver you like an airborne bell, its clangs
ill gut your heart, will keep
 their reverberant assault, no sleep

ll be the same again;
arked, muted by this inexorable hyphen
ou cannot be the same;
ere is no sanctuary, the god will come

d bed you in his plumage;
ent, bird-lidded, knotted in his rage
 lust he will flail down
ery abject appeal. . . . Quiet in gown

white the bride of Christ
oves down the waiting nave as if her wrist
re held and she led,
nds heart obeying the seeing unseen Dead,

d she led on as though
lking through shallow water, where the slow
e urges at her feet
 checks their driftwood longing. Will the sweet

n dedicated face,
ward as some old painting, find a place
 sweetest rest, a home
w in the Spirit's mansion and catacomb?

Will she encounter love,
Laughter, pain and grief, or will she live
For centuries encased
In waterglass serenity; the taste

Of an eternal death
In life upon her lips, although breath
Cannot fail? Her
Limbo holds her likes a fly in amber,

Beyond the reach of life.
Sisters, wastrels, when will you have enough
Of sacrifice and harm
And deprivation? Remember the mighty arm

That, white and sick with strain,
Wrestled the whole night out until the plain
Was light and he could see
Deep down the precipice of self, his adversary

And ask his blessing. Either
Make peace with yourselves, or live locked in such
As, ruinous from the start,
Turns dark with pity Jacob's brazen heart.

MERCEDES

Hopscotch
    Through patches
        Of light, a greeneyed
Dominican slanted
    From palm-frond street-shadow in
To a job, to stay on, to be safer;
But by June, daubed soap on her mirror:
Mercedes de la Rosa está muerta

Mercedes had
    Worked Casuarina-long days:

"San Francisco, San Francis-
Co, San Fran . . ." written fifty-three
Times . . . "In my grandmother's garden
Tomatoes grew, red whole
Hearts, we ate them; they said
   'Mercedes de la Rosa is dead' "

Dream-knives
   Cut out dolls—but I'll
   Help them—that leaf,
   Falling, is a dory . . .
   Chicago, Chicago;
Men: their pants
Pressed to the coil of a whip,
   Shoot billiard
   Eyes at me . . .
Merced es de la Rosa

I can hide my dolls, my
   Cuckoo-clock, though his beak
   Orders me to dance;
Sequins, I glue gold pieces, I sew
Justice on chiffon,
All colors—as I whirl,
   They dance—how my body aches!
   I must nail my cuckoo . . . The
Spinning mirror splinters:
   Mercy befits the Rose

Next day, duck with two heads,
Her radio quacked to itself; a needle
Slanted through the cuckoo's
   Heart; lint of chiffon
Rocked in Erzulie's breeze . . . "People
   Do strange sometimes," she had said,
   And,
Mercedes de la Rosa is dead

Robert Gardner

ISABELLA GARDNER was born in 1915 in Boston. She studied for the theatre and has acted professionally. She has been an editor for *Poetry* of Chicago, and has taught a poetry workshop for two years at the Y.M.C.A. Poetry Center. She has given readings at the Y.M. and Y.W.H.A. Poetry Center in New York, the Guggenheim Museum, the Library of Congress, and universities in the U.S., Italy, and London. She is the author of *Birthdays from the Ocean, The Looking Glass,* and *West of Childhood Poems 1950–1965*. She has a daughter and a son.

THE WIDOW'S YARD

"Snails lead slow idyllic lives" . . .
The rose and the laurel leaves
in the raw young widow's yard
were littered with silver. Hardly a leaf lacked the decimal scale
of the self of a snail. Frail
in friendship I observed with care
these creatures (meaning to spare
the widow's vulnerable eyes
the hurting pity in my gaze).

Snails, I said, are tender skinned.
Excess in nature . . . sun rain wind
are killers. To save themselves
snails shrink to shelter in their shells
where they wait safe and patient
until the elements are gent-
ler. And do they not have other foes?
the widow asked. Turtles crows
foxes rats, I replied, and canned
heat that picnickers abandon. Also parasites invade
their flesh and alien eggs are laid
inside their skins. Their mating
too is perilous. The meeting
turns their faces blue with bliss
and consummation of this
absolute embrace is so
extravagantly slow
in coming that love begun
at dawn may end in fatal sun.
The widow told me that her
husband knew snails' ways and his garden had been Eden for them. He
said the timid snail could lift three

times his weight straight up and haul
a wagon toy loaded with a whole
two hundred times his body's burden.
Then as we left the garden
she said that at the first faint chill
the first premonition of fall
the snails go straight to earth . . . excrete
the lime with which they then secrete
the opening in their shells . . . and wait for spring.
It is those little doors which sing,
she said, when they are boiled.
She smiled at me when I recoiled.

FALL IN MASSACHUSETTS

I saw the tall bush burn.
(Nineteen times a gallows-tree . . .
The tongue of fire muted by our guilt. There cannot be
a voice for deaf New Englanders vowed never to
    healed.)
I saw where a manna of flame had unfallowed the starv
    field
        where a witch charred
        where her bones roared
where each of the good-wives took her choice of holiday
    skewered house
and the mewing children barked another name
to their elders gathering apple-wood boughs
        and the sweet, the kindling fern:
        while cinders blew; and shame.

AT A SUMMER HOTEL

For my daughter,
Rose Van Kirk

I am here with my beautiful bountiful womanful child
to be soothed by the sea not roused by these roses roving
    wild.
My girl is gold in the sun and bold in the dazzling water,
she drowses on the blond sand and in the daisy fields my
    daughter
dreams. Uneasy in the drafty shade I rock on the veranda
reminded of Europa Persephone Miranda.

Martha Sanders

MAY SWENSON was born in Logan, Utah in 1919, the first child of immigrant Swedish parents. She graduated from Utah State University and shortly thereafter came to New York City. She has been an editor at New Directions, and her awards include a Guggenheim Fellowship and grants from the National Institute of Arts and Letters and the Ford Foundation. She has been a judge in poetry for the Lamont Selection of the Academy of American Poets and for the National Book Award, as well as writer-in-residence at Purdue University. Her experimental play, *The Floor*, was produced at the American Place Theatre in 1966. Her books of poetry include *Half Sun Half Sleep; Iconographs, To Mix with Time;* and *Poems to Solve,* a selection for young people; all published by Charles Scribner's Sons.

WOMEN

Women
should be
pedestals
moving
pedestals
moving
to the
motions
of men

Or they
should be
little horses
those wooden
sweet
oldfashioned
painted
rocking
horses

the gladdest things in the toyroom

The
pegs
of their
ears
so familiar
and dear
to the trusting
fists
to be chafed

feelingly
and then
unfeelingly
To be
joyfully
ridden
rockingly
ridden until
the restored

egos dismount and the legs stride away

nmobile
sweetlipped
sturdy
and smiling
women
should always
be waiting

willing
to be set
into motion
Women
should be
pedestals
to men

ALL THAT TIME

I saw two trees embracing.
One leaned on the other
as if to throw her down.
But she was the upright one.
Since their twin youth, maybe she
had been pulling him toward her
all that time,

and finally almost uprooted him.
He was the thin, dry, insecure one,
the most wind-warped, you could see.
And where their tops tangled
it looked like he was crying
on her shoulder.
On the other hand, maybe he

had been trying to weaken her,
break her, or at least
make her bend
over backwards for him
just a little bit.
And all that time
she was standing up to him

the best she could.
She was the most stubborn,
the straightest one, that's a fact.
But he had been willing
to change himself—
even if it was for the worse—
all that time.

At the top they looked like one
tree, where they were embracing.
It was plain they'd be

always together.
Too late now to part.
When the wind blew, you could hear
them rubbing on each other.

A COUPLE

A bee
rolls
in the yellow
rose.
Does she
invite his hairy
rub?

He scrubs
himself
in her creamy
folds;
a bullet, soft, imposes
her spiral and, spinning, burrows
to her dewy
shadows.

The gold
grooves almost
match
the yellow
bowl.
Does his touch
please
or scratch?

When he's
done
his honey-
thieving
at her matrix,

whirs free
leaving,
she
closes,
still
tall, chill,
unrumpled on her stem.

A FIXTURE

Women women women women
in a department store
with hats on (hats in *it*)
and shoes on (shoes in *it*)
dresses coats gloves on (and *in*
all the departments)

In the lobby (in a niche)
between two glass revolving doors
sluff sluff sluff sluff
(rubber bottoms of whirling doors)
flick flick click click
(women in women out) sits a nun

In the mid-whirl (a station)
white black wooden (a fixture)
holding a wooden cup she sits
between the glitter of double doors
hexagonal glasses glittering
over glassy fixed eyes

A garter snake of black
beads (wooden?) catching light
crawling (clicking) crawling
(clicking) up her draped
fixed short carved
black knees (thighs)

Her white hat (hood) a head cover
her shoes short black
flat (foot covers)
her dress a black curtain (cape)
over a longer curtain shape
she is the best dressed

MADELINE DeFREES was born in Ontario, Oregon in 1919, and spent her early years in the western part of the state, attending Marylhurst College and the University of Oregon, where she received her M.A. in 1951. A member of the Sisters of the Holy Name since 1936, she has taught in colleges of the Order, at Seattle University, and at the University of Washington. In 1967 she joined the creative writing program at the University of Montana, where she is an Associate Professor of English. Of her three books, published under the name of Sister Mary Gilbert, her book of poetry is *From the Darkroom*, Bobbs-Merrill, 1963.

LETTER TO AN ABSENT SON

right to call you son.   That cursing alcoholic
e god I married early before I really knew him:
ed to his crossbeam bed, I've lasted thirty years.
s are my habit now.   Without them I'm afraid.

ight I spider up the wall to hide in crevices
er than guilt.   His hot breath smokes me out.
l and fall into the arms I bargained for
g them cool as rain.   A flower touch could tame me.

g me down that giant beam to lie submissive
is fumbling clutch.   One touch.   Bad weather
es indoors: a cyclone takes me.

shall I find a shelter in the clouds, driven by
, gold breaking out of them everywhere?
ing is what it pretends.   It gathers to a loss
aves and graves.   Winter in the breath.
r father looked like you, his dying proportioned
y to my breast.   I boxed him in my plain pine
s and let him take his ease just for a minute.

THE WAKE

sitting on your Indian rock watching the third
go out, larger, in the ditch farther down.
n all those stricken wind chimes catch
e's snag tooth I am with you, pitched
a tuning fork to your stark room
lyde Street in the City of the Golden Gate.

nted to crash the gate.   Steady the night
beat your threatened ground.   A clutch
sengage old drives: that head under the wheel
e ocean road, turned helmet-white on the shoulder.

Asleep in a violent land, huge gears unlock.
The right sounds mesh, hand easy on the choke.

A shift into all weathers.   We talk of going out
to the engine's relaxed running.   The naked stand
on the soggy bath mat, everything slipping away
like a shoreline.   Or into manic wind, our dead-end
words blown back into our faces.   If people say,
"When she washed dishes like surf on Acapulco . . .

we'll lean into that legend, weathered beams shifting
everything moving out past the breakwater.   The older
of single lives, true as rock to lichen.   Covered by mo
than the lover's body, we let the pared moon haul us i
ride the hovercraft that barely touches water.   Sky fa
into the sea.   The dark wings past the window widen.

Herb Weitman

MONA VAN DUYN was born in 1921. Her poems
have appeared in literary magazines since 1942, and
her work has been included in six anthologies. Her
books are *Valentines to the Wide World, A Time of
Bees,* and *To See, To Take.* She is the co-founder
and co-editor of *Perspective, a Quarterly of Literature,* and she has taught at the University of Iowa
Writers' Workshop, the University of Louisville, and
Washington University College at St. Louis. Her
prizes include *Poetry*'s Eunice Tietjens Award, 1956;
Poetry Northwest's Helen Bullis Prize, 1964; *Poetry*'s
Harriet Monroe Award, 1968; the Hart Crane
Memorial Award, the American Weave Press,
1968; first prize, Borestone Mountain Anthol-
ogy, 1968; co-winner of the Bollingen Prize for *To
See, To Take,* which also won the National Book
Award for poetry in 1971; she has also received a
large grant from the National Council on the Arts.

DEATH BY AESTHETICS

Here is the doctor, an abstracted lover,
dressed as a virgin, coming to keep the tryst.
The patient was early; she is lovely; but yet
she is sick, his instruments will agree on this.

Is this the place, she wonders, and is he the one?
Yes, love is the healer, he will strip her bare,
and all his machinery of definition
tells her experience is costly here,

so she is reassured. The doctor approaches
and bends to her heart. But she sees him sprout like a
with metallic twigs on his fingers and blooms of chrom
at his eye and ear for the sterile ceremony.

Oh tight and tighter his rubber squeeze of her arm.
"Ahhh" she sighs at a chilly touch on her tongue.
Up the tubes her breath comes crying, as over her,
back and breast, he moves his silver thumb.

His fluoroscope hugs her. Soft the intemperate girl,
disordered. Willing she lies while he unfolds
her disease, but a stem of glass protects his fingertips
from her heat, nor will he catch her cold.

He peels her. Under the swaddling epiderm
her body is the same blue bush. Beautiful canals
course like a postcard scene that's sent him often.
He counts the *tiptup, tiptup* of her dutiful valves.

Pain hides like a sinner in her mesh of nerves.
But her symptoms constellate! Quickly he warms
to his consummation, while her fever flares
in its wick of vein, her wicked blood burns.

hands her a paper. "Goodbye. Live quietly,
ke some new friends. I've seen these stubborn cases
ed with time. My bill will arrive. Dear lady,
been a most enjoyable diagnosis."

clings, but her fingers slip on his starchy dress.
on't leave me! Learn me! If this is all, you've swindled
whole booty of meaning, where is my dearness?
re against pore, the delicate hairs commingled,

h cells and ligaments, tissue lapped on bone,
et me, feel the way my body feels,
d in my bounty of dews, fluxes and seasons,
fices, in my wastes and smells

self. Self in the secret stones I chafed
shape in my bladder. Out of a dream I fished
ache that feeds in my stomach's weedy slough.
is tender swelling's the bud of my frosted wish.

rch out my mind's embroidery of scars.
ichor runs to death so speedily,
t up your text and taste my living texture.
eat to hunt me with love, and burn with me."

t he is gone. "Don't touch me," was all he answered.
eparateness," says the paper. The world, we beg,
keep her though she's caught its throbbing senses,
bugs still swim in her breath, she's bright with its plague.

From: THREE VALENTINES
TO THE WIDE WORLD

III

"Your yen two wol slee me sodenly;
I may the beautee of hem not sustene."
Merciles Beaute

When, in the middle of my life, the earth stalks me
with sticks and stones, I fear its merciless beauty.
This morning a bird woke me with a four-note outcry
and cried out eighteen times. With the shades down, sle
as I was, I recognized his agony.
It resembles ours. With one more heave, the day
sends us a generous orb and lets us see
all sights lost when we lie down finally.

And if, in the middle of her life, some beauty falls on
a girl, who turns under its swarm to astonished woman
then, into that miraculous buzzing, stung
in the lips and eyes without mercy, strangers may run.
An untended power—I pity her and them.
It is late, late; haste! says the falling moon,
as blinded they stand and smart till the fever's done
and blindly she moves, wearing her furious weapon.

Beauty is merciless and intemperate.
Who, turning this way and that, by day, by night,
still stands in the heart-felt storm of its benefit,
will plead in vain for mercy, or cry, "Put out
the lovely eyes of the world, whose rise and set
move us to death!" And never will temper it,
but against that rage slowly may learn to pit
love and art, which are compassionate.

From: RECOVERY

III. A Memory

'rite a letter to Grandpa," my mother said, but he
   smelled old.

e'll give you something nice," she said, but I was afraid.

 never looked at me, he muttered to himself, and he hid

1 things to drink all over his house, and Grandma cried.

gray stranger with a yellowed mustache, why should I
   have mailed

 very first message to him? Well, consider the innocent
   need

t harries us all: "Your Aunt Callie thinks she's smart,
   but *her* kid

er sent her first letter to Pa." (To hold her I had to be
   good.)

ou've learned to write. Write Grandpa!" she said, so I
   did.

vas hard work. "Dear Grandpa, How are you, I am
   fine,"

 I couldn't come to the end of a word when I came
   to the margin,

 the lines weren't straight on the page. I erased that
   paper so thin

 could almost see through it in spots. I couldn't seem
   to learn

ook ahead. (Mother, remember we both had to win.)

e are coming to visit you next Sunday if it does not
   rain.

rs truly, your loving granddaughter, Mona Van Duyn."

t Sunday he took me aside and gave me the biggest coin

er had, and I ran away from the old man.

"Look, Mother, what Grandpa gave me. And as soon a
    get back home
I'll write him again for another half dollar." But Moth
    said "Shame!"
and so I was ashamed. But I think at that stage of t
    game,
or any stage of the game, things are almost what they see
and the exchange was fair. Later in the afternoon I caug
    him.
"Medicine," he said, but he must have known his chanc
    were slim.
People don't hide behind the big fern, I wasn't dumb,
and I was Grandma's girl. "So, *Liebling,* don't tell then
he said, but that sneaky smile called me by my real nan

Complicity I understood. What human twig isn't bent
by the hidden weight of its wish for some strict covenan
"Are you going to tell?" he wanted to know, and I sa
    "No, I won't."
He looked right at me and straightened his mouth and sa
    "So, *Kind,*
we fool them yet," and it seemed to me I knew what
    meant.
Then he reached in his pocket and pulled out two cand
    covered with lint,
and we stood there and each sucked one. "*Ja,* us two,
    know what we want."
When he leaned down to chuck my chin I caught my fi
    Grandpa-scent.
Oh, it was a sweet seduction on pillows of peppermint!

And now, in the middle of life, I'd like to learn how
    forgive
the heart's grandpa, mother and kid, the hard ways
    have to love.

RELATIONSHIPS

The legal children of a literary man
remember his ugly words to their mother.
He made them keep quiet and kissed them later.
He made them stop fighting and finish their supper.
His stink in the bathroom sickened their noses.
He left them with sitters in lonesome houses.
He mounted their mother and made them wear braces.
He fattened on fame and raised them thin.

But the secret sons of the same man
spring up like weeds from the seed of his word.
They eat from his hand and it is not hard.
They unravel his sweater and swing from his beard.
They smell in their sleep his ferns and roses.
They hunt the fox on his giant horses.
They slap their mother, repeating his phrases,
and swell in his sight and suck him thin.

Morton Sacks

RUTH WHITMAN was born in 1922. She is the winner of the Alice Fay di Castagnola Award, the Kovner Award, and the *Massachusetts Review* Jennie Tane Award. She was a Fellow in Translation and Poetry at the Radcliffe Institute for two years, and she is presently teaching a poetry workshop at Radcliffe and is Director of the Poetry Writing Program in the schools under the Massachusetts Council on the Arts and the National Endowment. She is the author of *Blood & Milk Poems* (1963), *The Passion of Lizzie Borden: New and Selected Poems* (1972), the editor and translator of *An Anthology of Modern Yiddish Poetry* (1966), and the editor of *The Selected Poems of Jacob Glatstein* (1972), all published by October House. Harcourt brought out *The Marriage Wig* in 1968.

SHE DOESN'T WANT TO BRING
THE TIDES IN ANY MORE

Every time she tugs the sun across the sky
some old wound
comes apart at the seams.
But housekeeping by the clock means keeping
every star prompt. She puffs along,
blowing a strand of graying hair out of her eyes,
but she gets each planet to its place
in time. She bruises a hip
moving all this furniture around.

She steers clouds, fans winds, and slices
or mends the moon, according to the day.
Worst of all is bringing in the tides.
One hand brings them in on one side,
the other pushes them away;
                              while her knee
keeps the tipped earth spinning on its axis
precariously.

No wonder she went away and sat down on a sand dune,
wishing she were grass.
If she sits still long enough,
rain will come to her.

IN THE SMOKING CAR

That hatless chewed woman sending me messages
with her eyes, what does she know about me?
That I've had my last child, that my
clocks are stopping? That love still comes to me
like birthdays or Christmas, and a brushed kiss
can be a whole concert?

She is grayer than I, more toothless,
but she grins like a sister.
Do my sins show?
                    What deception
does she see through me?
I shrink from her wrinkles, her sporty air,
her certain knowledge, older than cats,
that I am pretending, pretending, pretending.

CUTTING THE JEWISH BRIDE'S HAIR

It's to possess more than the skin
that those old world Jews
exacted the hair of their brides.
        Good husband, lover of the Torah,
        does the calligraphy of your bride's hair
        interrupt your page?

Before the clownish friction of flesh
creating out of nothing
a mockup of its begetters,
a miraculous puppet of God,
you must first divorce her from her vanity.

She will snip off her pride,
cut back her appetite to be devoured,
she will keep herself well braided,
her love's furniture will not endanger you,
        but this little amputation
        will shift the balance of the universe.

Rollie McKenna

DENISE LEVERTOV was born in 1923 in England of Russian-Jewish and Welsh parents. She published her first book, *The Double Image,* Cresset Press, in England in 1946. She came to the U.S. in 1948 with her American husband, Mitch Goodman, an editor and novelist. She has taught at various places, including CCNY, Berkeley and MIT. She has one son, Nikolai, an artist. The latest of her volumes of poetry include *Relearning the Alphabet* and *To Stay Alive,* from New Directions.

THE MUTES

Those groans men use
passing a woman on the street
or on the steps of the subway

to tell her she is a female
and their flesh knows it,

are they a sort of tune,
an ugly enough song, sung
by a bird with a slit tongue

but meant for music?

Or are they the muffled roaring
of deafmutes trapped in a building that is
slowly filling with smoke?

Perhaps both.

Such men most often
look as if groan were all they could do,
yet a woman, in spite of herself,

knows it's a tribute:
if she were lacking all grace
they'd pass her in silence:

so it's not only to say she's
a warm hole. It's a word

in grief-language, nothing to do with
primitive, not an ur-language;
language stricken, sickened, cast down

in decrepitude. She wants to
throw the tribute away, dis-
gusted, and can't,

it goes on buzzing in her ear,
it changes the pace of her walk,
the torn posters in echoing corridors

spell it out, it
quakes and gnashes as the train comes in.
Her pulse sullenly

had picked up speed,
but the cars slow down and
jar to a stop while her understanding

keeps on translating:
'Life after life after life goes by

without poetry,
without seemliness,
without love.'

IN MIND

There's in my mind a woman
of innocence, unadorned but

fair-featured, and smelling of
apples or grass. She wears

a utopian smock or shift, her hair
is light brown and smooth, and she

is kind and very clean without
ostentation—
                but she has
no imagination.
                And there's a
turbulent moon-ridden girl

or old woman, or both,
dressed in opals and rags, feathers

and torn taffeta,
who knows strange songs—

but she is not kind.

From: TWO VARIATIONS

Enquiry

You who go out on schedule
to kill, do you know
there are eyes that watch you,
eyes whose lids you burned off,
that see you eat your steak
and buy your girlflesh
and sell your PX goods
and sleep?
She is not old,
she whose eyes
know you.
She will outlast you.
She saw
her five young children
writhe and die;
in that hour
she began to watch you,
she whose eyes are open forever.

AN EMBROIDERY

Rose Red's hair is brown as fur
and shines in firelight as she prepares
supper of honey and apples, curds and whey,

for the bear, and leaves it ready
on the hearth-stone.

Rose White's grey eyes
look into the dark forest.

Rose Red's cheeks are burning,
sign of her ardent, joyful
compassionate heart.
Rose White is pale,
turning away when she hears
the bear's paw on the latch.

When he enters, there is
frost on his fur,
he draws near to the fire
giving off sparks.

Rose White catches the scent of the forest,
of mushrooms, of rosin.

Together Rose Red and Rose White
sing to the bear;
it is a cradle song, a loom song,
a song about marriage, about
a pilgrimage to the mountains
long ago.
            Raised on an elbow,
the bear stretched on the hearth
nods and hums; soon he sighs
and puts down his head.

He sleeps; the Roses
bank the fire.
Sunk in the clouds of their feather bed
they prepare to dream.

Rose Red in a cave that smells of honey
dreams she is combing the fur of her cubs

with a golden comb.
Rose White is lying awake.

Rose White shall marry the bear's brother.
Shall he too
when the time is ripe,
step from the bear's hide?
Is that other, her bridegroom,
here in the room?

THE ACHE OF MARRIAGE

The ache of marriage:

thigh and tongue, beloved,
are heavy with it,
it throbs in the teeth

We look for communion
and are turned away, beloved,
each and each

It is leviathan and we
in its belly
looking for joy, some joy
not to be known outside it

two by two in the ark of
the ache of it.

DESPAIR

At David's Grave
for B. and H. F.

While we were visiting David's grave
I saw at a little distance

a woman hurrying towards another grave
hands outstretched, stumbling

in her haste; who then
fell at the stone she made for

and lay sprawled upon it, sobbing,
sobbing and crying out to it.

She was neatly dressed in a pale coat
and seemed neither old nor young.

I couldn't see her face, and my friends
seemed not to know she was there.

Not to distress them, I said nothing.
But she was not an apparition.

And when we walked
back to the car in silence

I looked stealthily back and saw she rose
and quieted herself and began slowly

to back away from the grave.
Unlike David, who lives

in our lives, it seemed
whoever she mourned dwelt

there, in the field, under stone.
It seemed the woman

believed whom she loved heard her,
heard her wailing, observed

the nakedness of her anguish,
and would not speak.

Marlis Schwieger

DAISY ALDAN's books of poetry include *The Destruction of Cathedrals & Other Poems, Seven: Seven, The Masks Are Becoming Faces, Breakthrough: Poems in a new medium, Love Poems of Daisy Aldan* and *Of Arrows and Vectors*. She has translated poems by Stéphane Mallarmé and Albert Steffen, as well as a play in verse by Albert Steffen, *The Death Experience of Manes*. From 1954 to 1959 she was the editor of *Folder Magazine of Literature & Art*, and during the 60's American editor of *Two Cities*, a bilingual literary magazine published in Paris. She has also edited *Poems from India* and *A New Folder: Americans—Poems & Drawings*. She received the Poetry Forum Award for 1970 and now teaches creative writing at the School of Art & Design in New York City.

SNOW IN SUMMER

What just streamed outward from that midsummer center
    not periphery?
Snow? White now falling toward us, entering the room
    crystallizing.
Over and over I am not prepared for sudden white silences
color of death, flowers and butterflies freezing, changing
    without sequence.
Tied to you by this rope, grasping this crag, suspended
    over a glacial
cave worn smooth and dark by ages of molding ice, will
    I become sculpture?

A long time ago, yesterday, the cows had such nice faces
    they allowed
us to pet them, brush flies from their eyes: they kissed
    us with their big rough tongues.
In high mounds of flowers, deer stood in green and gold
    mist beneath two rainbows.
Today, those glacial hours of waiting, mounting snow
    blocking the door,
the untraversable waterfalls taking over the clayey road
the heartbeat irregular in the altitude growing more
    rarefied.

Lying day of white snow-veils and cloud drapes, low almost
    to the ground,
time grown measureless where a last hope expires and
    we become history
not presence. This silence, this ice-lance: mute paralysis
    setting in.
—I summoned this snow for you,—you said. And I:—
    will bring you frozen
flowers from the cemetery because you understand
    murder.—

AM MOVED BY A NECESSITY FROM WITHIN

he road to your house leads past the motley plane trees,
 the bongo-playing carpenters who corrupt the street
f new buildings; the fountain of the muscular angel,
  and the Old Casino where Fats Domino still moans;
  past the Port

here the old men sit on the walls waiting for death.
 I await the number SEVEN bus, and it arrives
ke a last dice throw. The sun is hot on the pavement
  and the roofs.
  The shopgirls are still riding home for lunch, though
  I have crossed

vo oceans, and time, and will cross them again.
 We pass the shop of the magician mechanic,
e Market of the Masked Faces and Wigs, near the river
  of the parched white rocks where a brass cockerel
  crows:

–irregular rectangles, the rows of stalls
 by the railing. *You* waving from the ramp we move
nder? bending over papayas? at the wine-seller's
  booth? (I am moved by a necessity from within.)

here is the park of the wrinkled women in black.
 Sudden altar-cold, the clouds ragged. You are three
  streets
om here. The terrace; the awning orange and blue, the
  bird-cage.
  There is the family of the porcelain toilet seats;

ur hallway. I place a note in your box
 with a number, run, hide near a plane tree, eyes
  glued

to the wall of brick and glass behind which you mov
      the doorway.
      The Man with the Square Face passes; motions: I
      still,   still . . .

And   you   appear! laughing. Earthquake! Escap
      I hug the buildings, dash into the Algerian
cafe, (Is this a spy film?),   order a whiskey;   wait un
      you pass.   Then slip out and catch the SEVEN bad
      to the hotel.

BESMILR BRIGHAM was born in Pace, Mississippi,
September 28, 1923. Her great grandfather was a
Choctaw Indian. She studied at the New School for
Social Research in New York, and now lives in
Horatio, Arkansas. Her anthology publications in-
clude *31 New American Poets, New Directions #21*
and *#23, Best Poems of 1970, New Generation:
Poetry* and *Their Place in the Heat, Contemporary
Poetry Statements.* Her book of poems, *Heaved from
the Earth,* was published by Alfred A. Knopf in 1971.
She has also received a fellowship grant from the
National Endowment for the Arts.

THE TINY
BABY LIZARD

wiggling head-first from the egg
down in a burrow
hole made hard and soft in the dirt, the wise
lizard creature mother
hatching her eggs

the belly of her body
warm he runs over the still startling color
moving head, reaching down
drapes over her neck between legs curls
a long curl string
in the coiled curve of her flesh, the body

lying in the dark
her alert calmed head, not darting
not slithering as they do in the open rushed
from fear, weed ways and rock ways

he learns first the quiver quiet
flesh-way
earth-instinct circumference
he eats from her mouth

WHEN COTTON HAYMES
WALKS DOWN THE STREET

when Cotton Haymes gets into his police car
he has to shift over his billy club, like a man
shifting his pants
dancing, close to a girl,—that way. his gun
his club he walks
his eyes don't look at you, in the face

but he looks at your shape, man, woman
as though he could know/tell
an intention.   he walks herding the bare street
and all move away from him

      he has learned from a walk that a man is
guilty.   at every corner he passes a suspect, sniffing
the pavement, parked cars
he knows the cars he knows the streets, who
is in town, who isn't
when he lies down to sleep with his billy club
he raises before us, his guilt
raises with his hands following his dreams

WHAT IS SHE TRYING TO DO,
TO PATTERN LOVE

   to cut a shape out in form of a man
   simply, as she cuts a dress
   to make it
   quickly
   the way she sits up all night sewing

   whipping the hems in
   a new dress to wear Sundays
   to dance
   before his eyes
   in sparkles of shape and long line, color
   the short white skirt

   pleated at the knees
   to walk
   before him a quiet flirtatious child
   and sleep the night after
   dreaming

she has many threads
she works
with rainbows of variation, her eyes
catch her own place in the glass.   she is

still a girl
the pain
as her hands work on the cloth, a child-girl
waiting.   as she moves her still hands
innocently, before his thought

MOUNTAINS

the women dream of
snake and lizard
they sleep with black warrior

the ridges spread
like weeping dinosaurs
long bone
skeletons
above their green blankets

warped bones
struck up white in cold and filled with
skeletons of women
a woman flung her hair out weeping
the great still female form the shoulders
haunched down
moves us—
covering her hard mature breasts
the mountain piled dead with
war arrows
set clean with weeping

women abandoned
left to their keeping

alone, hovered over with loneliness
their backs held thrown (without claim

graves among aloes and iris
graves among willows

like left old men
carving out intricate snake heads of war—
washing in the rain
quiet a cemetery of great sad peaks
cemetery of dinosaur and snakes that
crawl, turtle heads

the snake head where there is no snake
pyramids
dripping their slaughter
with forgotten blood

altered with the dead, weeping with anger

BARBARA GUEST, born in North Carolina in 1923, and educated at the University of California, has lived in New York City since 1949. She is connected with the abstract expressionists both as a reviewer for periodicals and through friendships. She received the Yaddo Award in 1958 and has been anthologized in *New American Poetry, Penguin Book of American Poetry, Another World, Les Jeunes Poètes Américains,* and *American Poets in a Japanese Anthology.* Her books of poetry include *Location of Things, Poems, The Blue Stairs,* and *Lithographs of I Ching,* poems with lithographs by Sheila Ishani. She also writes plays.

SAFE FLIGHTS

To no longer like the taste of whisky
This is saying also no to you who are
A goldfinch in the breeze,
To no longer wish winter to have explanations
To lace your shoes in the snow
With no need to remember,
To no longer pull the two blankets
Over your shoulders, to no longer feel the cold,
To no longer pretend in the flower
There is a secret, or in the earth a tomb,
And no longer water on stone hurting the ear,
Making those five noises of thunder
And you tremble no longer.
To no longer travel over mountains,
Over small farms
No longer the weather changing and the atmosphere
Causing delicate breaks where the nerves confuse,
To no longer have your name shouted
And your birthmark again described,
To no longer fear where the rapids break
A miniature rock under your canoe,
To no longer repeat the mirror is water,
The house is a burden to the weak cyclone,
You are under a tent where promises perform
And the ring you grasp as an aerialist
Glides, no longer.

SAVING TALLOW

'isible tallow of the hurricane night
in fair candle
  yacht cradling
ie room's deep water

        where the wave

raises

> its sail

a procession

> of shoulders

the falling olives

> on yellow knees

and cities

> drowned

in their comet clothing

> dragged from the sea

> Candle!

lone palm tree   lonely diver
covered with sea lice

> most vertical

the room dedicates its curves to you.

> There was once a shadow

called Luis; there was once an eyebrow
whose name was Domingo.   Once there
were children, grown-ups, organs;
there were moving legs and there was
speech.   In the daylight there were
small whimpers made by the African cat;
in the candlelight there were couplings
of such sonority evening callers
merely left their cards; no one drew back
the curtains; there were no curtains
the candlelight fell on grass and
like a candle up stood the water hose.

> There were many mathematical

forms

> the obliquity of a painting
> her mouth drawn by a corner

transverses on the arrow light

> where the smile flies off

at the room's center a hair part

> the nose of a window
> louvered as coral rock
> where a person walked

was sleepy
must be awakened
or adorations and questions

is marine
related to the diving fish

Take me on your dolphin skin!

I shall be absent soon!

aving the tallow with capable hands
eizing with the loyal closed eyes of foliage

Puff

SHIRLEY KAUFMAN was born in 1923 in Seattle, Washington. She won the Academy of American Poets Prize from San Francisco State College in 1964; she was in the Discovery Program of the Poetry Center, the Y.M. and Y.W.H.A., New York, in 1967, and was United States winner of the International Poetry Forum in 1969. Her book, *The Floor Keeps Turning,* from the University of Pittsburgh Press, was a National Council of the Arts Selection for 1970. Her work has been included in *Quickly Aging Here* and *Best Poems* of 1965, 1966, and 1969. She has translated from the Hebrew a book-length poem, *My Little Sister,* by the Israeli poet Abba Kovner, published by Penguin in its Modern European Poets' Series in 1971.

HER GOING

As if I carried a charm
for daughters, I would carve a smile
each day and enter it, set it
between us like a pumpkin glowing.
Out of its hollow mouth,
the candle burned away.

No one will smooth her now
with promises. But when the sun comes
through the glass, I see her face,
smell the milky wrinkle of her skin,
feel the small shape of light
going out of my arms.

THE HUNGER ARTIST

"If I had found it, believe me, I should
have made no fuss and stuffed myself like
you or anyone else."

Franz Kafka

I

It's no use trying to find again
what it was like.
And the spectacle of it. The breasts
begin to go, skin
loosens under the chin.
You watch
an aging courtesan undress.

2

Him waiting, waiting as if
you never loved by night.

Long welts
of daylight, another bed.
To let it happen
easy as Eden, no wringing
of the mind, wrestle of leaves
to squeeze through.
His solemn arms, his room
not dark enough, your having
to be the way you are.
You fasten like things on a pond
to their own reflection.
Till he discovers that
you cannot play.

3

Remember your swimming
when a wave fell in.
Too stunned to fight the undertow,
you gave yourself up
dreaming to the pull.
When you lie down once more
in dangerous places
taking the fruit between your teeth,
there is always the light
thatched over another
who breathes beside you, entire,
strange to your wanting
even the least of what he was.

4

When plastic chairs in the kitchen
begin to crack, or fabric
on the footstool wears
through to the stuffing,
or the sink falls slowly down

from the level of the formica counter
because water got in
under the unseen wood and is secretly
chewing it all away;

when you look in the mirror
after everyone leaves in the morning,
and the only sound is the thin hum
of the furnace, and suddenly
it stops, and the house begins to tick,
and you see the small wrinkles

under your lashes smudged
with mascara you never get off,
and you make a terrible smile
watching them deepen and lengthen
like thin lines raked in the sand
of a perfect Japanese garden;

you feel everything
being eaten from its surface.
Soon there will be no covers
and what is under
will be exposed, wasted,
no longer able
to keep the flesh alive.

MOTHERS, DAUGHTERS

Through every night we hate,
preparing the next day's
war. She bangs the door.
Her face laps up my own
despair, the sour, brown eyes,
the heavy hair she won't
tie back. She's cruel,

as if my private meanness
found a way to punish us.
We gnaw at each other's
skulls. Give me what's mine.
I'd haul her back, choking
myself in her, herself
in me. There is a book
called *Poisons* on her shelf.
Her room stinks with incense,
animal turds, hamsters
she strokes like silk. They
exercise on the bathroom
floor, and two drop through
the furnace vent. The whole
house smells of the accident,
the hot skins, the small
flesh rotting. Six days
we turn the gas up then
to fry the dead. I'd fry
her head if I could until
she cried love, love me!

All she won't let me do.
Her stringy figure in
the windowed room shares
its thin bones with no one.
Only her shadow on the glass
waits like an older sister.
Now she stalks, leans forward,
concentrates merely on getting
from here to there. Her feet
are bare. I hear her breathe
where I can't get in. If I
break through to her, she will
drive nails into my tongue.

APPLES

No use waiting for it to stop
raining in my face like a wet towel,
having to catch a plane,
to pick the apples from her tree
and bring them home.

The safest place to be
is under the branches. She
in her bed and her mouth
dry in the dry room.
Don't go out in the rain.

I stretch my arms for apples
anyway, feel how the ripe ones
slide in my hands like cups
that want to be perfect. Juices
locked up in the skin.

She used to slice them in quarters,
cut through the core,
open the inside out. Fingers
steady on the knife, expert
at stripping things.

Sometimes she split them sideways
into halves to let a star break
from the center with tight seeds,
because I wanted that,
six petals in the flesh.

Flavor of apples inhaled as flowers,
not even biting them.
Apples at lunch or after school
like soup, a fragrance rising
in the steam, eat and be well.

I bring the peeled fruit to her
where she lies, carve it
in narrow sections, celery white,
place them between her fingers,
Mother, eat. And be well.

Sit where her brown eyes
empty out the light, watching
her mind slip backwards
on the pillow, swallowing
apples, swallowing her life.

LISEL MUELLER was born February 8, 1924 in
Hamburg, Germany. She came to this country in
1939, and now lives with her husband and two
daughters in Lake Forest, Illinois. Her books of
poetry include *Dependencies,* University of North
Carolina Press (1965), *Life of a Queen,* Juniper
Press (1970), and *Voyages to the Inland Sea* (with
Dave Etter and John Knoepfle), Center for Con-
temporary Poetry, Wisconsin State University at La
Crosse (1971).

LIFE OF A QUEEN

Childhood

For two days her lineage is in doubt,
then someone deciphers the secret message.
They build a pendulous chamber
for her, and stuff her with sweets.

Workers keep bringing her royal jelly.
She knows nothing of other lives,
about digging in purple crocus
and round-dances in the sun.

Poor and frail little rich girl,
she grows immense in her hothouse.
Whenever she tries to stop eating,
they open her mouth and force it down.

The Flight

She marries him in mid-air;
    for a moment
he is ennobled, a prince.

She gives the signal
    for their embrace;
over too soon. O, nevermore.

She is bathed, curtains are drawn.
    Ten thousand lives
settle inside her belly.

Now to the only labor she knows.
    She remembers
nothing of him, or their fall.

The Recluse

They make it plain
her term is over.
No one comes;
they let her starve.

The masses, her children,
whip up sweets
for a young beauty
who is getting fat.

Nothing to do.
Her ovaries paper,
her sperm sac dust,
she shrivels away.

A crew disassembles
her royal cell.
Outside, a nation
crowns its queen.

A NUDE BY EDWARD HOPPER

For Margaret Gaul

The light
drains me of what I might be,
a man's dream
of heat and softness;
or a painter's
—breasts cozy pigeons,
arms gently curved
by a temperate noon.

I am
blue veins, a scar,
a patch of lavender cells,
used thighs and shoulders;
my calves
are as scant as my cheeks,
my hips won't plump
small, shimmering pillows:

but this body
is home, my childhood
is buried here, my sleep
rises and sets inside,
desire
crested and wore itself thin
between these bones—
I live here.

THE MERMAID

All day he had felt her stirring
under the boat, and several times
when the net had tightened, frog-nervous,
he had bungled the pulling-in,
half-glad of the stupid, open mouths
he could throw back.
                              At sundown
the shifting and holding of time and air
had brought her to the still surface,
to sun herself in the last, slow light
where lilies and leeches tangled and rocked.
He could have taken her then, aimed his net
as dragonfly hunters do when the glassy gliding
of rainbows goes to their heads,
could have carried her home on tiptoe
and lifted her lightly, ever so lightly,
over his sill.

And, hopeless, knew
that to have her alive was only this:
the sounding, casting, waiting, seeing
and praying the light not to move,
not yet to round the bay of her shoulder
and passing, release her
to the darkness he would not enter.

VASSAR MILLER was born in Houston, Texas,
July 1924. She received her B.A. and M.A. degrees
from the University of Houston. Her books of poetry
include *Adam's Footprint, Wage War on Silence,*
which was nominated for the Pulitzer Prize, *My
Bones Being Wiser,* and *Onions and Roses.* She has
traveled over much of the United States and in
Europe, and is presently living in Houston where she
has conducted tutorial courses in creative writing at
St. John's School.

REGRET

Had you come to me
as I to you once
with naked asking,
I should have let you.
We should have slept,
two arrows bound together
wounding no one.
Instead, you chose to lie
set to the bow of your own darkness.

METAMORPHOSES

ou kissed her, and I watched you for a moment
ridled to your desire, tamed to the will of the woods,
the way of the wilds, your urbane grace
ittish and shy compared to the creature come down to
     drink of her beauty by dusk.
nd I thought for a moment how
y body might be other than itself—
proper parts be banks whereon you rested,
oves wherein you sheltered, pastures where you
     pleasured,
y speaking be the flow and ravel of its lines
aping, cascading, sharply declining downward,
ened into the pool of shadow wherein you dived at
     leisure.

nd under your kiss that it could not feel
y flesh, dispassionate stick beside you, startled
ck to its formal freedom.

SPINSTER'S LULLABY

For Jeff

Clinging to my breast, no stronger
Than a small snail snugly curled,
Safe a moment from the world,
Lullaby a little longer.

Wondering how one tiny human
Resting so, on toothpick knees
In my scraggly lap, gets ease,
I rejoice, no less a woman

With my nipples pinched and dumb
To your need whose one word's sucking.
Never mind, though. To my rocking
Nap a minute, find your thumb

While I gnaw a dream and nod
To the gracious sway that settles
Both our hearts, imperiled petals
Trembling on the pulse of God.

Jay K. Klein

SONYA DORMAN, born in 1924 in New York City, was raised on Cape Ann in Massachusetts, which she considers her "psychic home." She spent one year at a county agricultural school where she studied animal husbandry. She has been a writing instructor, a cook on a tuna boat, a receptionist, and a flamenco dancer. She is married and has one daughter. Her written work includes two short novels, short stories, and speculative fiction. She studied poetry with Stanley Kunitz, and her first book, *Poems,* published by Ohio State University Press in 1970, was a National Council on the Arts selection. She has completed an experimental novel and is working on a new poetry collection.

141

DECORATING PROBLEM

She came from country closed
only by stone walls to marry
into a house where the rooms
were proofed against breath,
words, fingers, and other pryers.
Beating about their door, her hands
bled from each honest callus,
all over the silent brocade.

Drapes were shut to protect
her face and the carpets,
no light was allowed to wilt
wax leaves or crewel roses.
In this arrangement she faded badly
until they realized her taste
for sun clashed with their scheme.

Seeing her hands die in awkward bunches
they divorced her from their grove
of lamps, repainted in gold
and ecru, bought her a ticket punched
for home and a pair of nice gloves.

IN THE SLY GARDENS

for Kurt and Evie

I

Veronica's lost in the garden
of tease, in love with fragrance
of love, stretching out of her tub
for a change and wearing a bell
in her hanging head. The wind
is undoing Veronica's hair, her face

is unfolding its mouth in the ferns.
Veronica's toes reach through the ends
of her shoes, and worms embroider
her scarf with proper mottoes.

2

Smiles open in the garden
of fangs where dogs of love
are lying low. Sometimes: a bristling
of pines. In the intervals
a feather settles where an egg
might have been. As soft as that.
The garden's inclinations turn
to light and wake knee-deep
in growls; the lawn gives tongue
and hungrily words point the bird.

3

In the sly gardens ferrets puzzle
the ways of mice; ho! the maze
a mole has wrought between the iron
roots of oak and beech. Behind
the gardener's back the grass like hair
grows on its ends and squirrels spiral
down the hollows of the lively tree.
The old man tweaking up the weeds
is out of bounds to all these gaining
ways: his shadow doesn't move for years.

HUNTERS

Where the owl
sheds a feather
I walk softly.
Across my back

is written the license
to kill.
If I love in the city
I'm lucky, but light
takes the long way down;
the street is a place
to die.
At night
the owl flies off to hunt.
I can hear the cry
of his catch
and a siren in the city,
where if you've no passion
for killing, nothing assuages
your hunger.
I keep to the forest,
my thought fletched
with a dark feather
aimed at the bird
I love.

Thomas Victor

CAROLYN KIZER was born in Spokane, Washington in 1925. She is editor and founder of *Poetry Northwest* and director of literary programs for the National Endowment for the Arts. Her books of poems include *Knock upon Silence*, *The Ungrateful Garden*, and most recently *Midnight Was My Cry*, published by Doubleday. She also writes fiction.

FOR JAN, IN BAR MARIA

Though it's true we were young girls when we met,
We have been friends for twenty-five years.
But we still swim strongly, run up the hill from the beach
    without getting too winded.
Here we idle in Ischia, a world away from our birthplace—
That colorless town!—drinking together, sisters of summer.
Now we like to have groups of young men gathered around
    us.
We are trivial-hearted. We don't want to die any more.

Remember, fifteen years ago, in our twin pinafores
We danced on the boards of the ferry dock at Mukilteo
Mad as yearling mares in the full moon?
Here in the morning moonlight we climbed on a workman's
    cart
And three young men, shouting and laughing, dragged it up
    through the streets of the village.
It is said we have shocked the people of Forio.
They call us Janna and Carolina, those two mad *straniere.*

PRO FEMINA

for Robert and Rolfe

One

From Sappho to myself, consider the fate of women.
How unwomanly to discuss it! Like a noose or an albatross
    necktie
The clinical sobriquet hangs us: cod-piece coveters.
Never mind these epithets; I myself have collected some
    honeys.
Juvenal set us apart in denouncing our vices
Which had grown, in part, from having been set apart
Women abused their spouses, cuckolded them, even plotted
To poison them. Sensing, behind the violence of his
    manner—

"Think I'm crazy or drunk?"—his emotional stake in us,
As we forgive Strindberg and Nietzsche, we forgive all
    those
Who cannot forget us. We *are* hyenas. Yes, we admit it.

While men have politely debated free will, we have howled
    for it,
Howl still, pacing the centuries, tragedy heroines.
Some who sat quietly in the corner with their embroidery
Were Defarges, stabbing the wool with the names of their
    ancient
Oppressors, who ruled by the divine right of the male—
I'm impatient of interruptions! I'm aware there were
    millions
Of mutes for every Saint Joan or sainted Jane Austen,
Who, vague-eyed and acquiescent, worshiped God as a
    man.
I'm not concerned with those cabbageheads, not truly
    feminine
But neutered by labor. I mean real women, like *you* and
    like *me*.

Freed in fact, not in custom, lifted from furrow and
    scullery,
Not obliged, now, to be the pot for the annual chicken,
Have we begun to arrive in time? With our well-known
Respect for life because it hurts so much to come out with
    it;
Disdainful of "sovereignty," "national honor" and other
    abstractions;

We can say, like the ancient Chinese to successive waves
    of invaders,
Relax, and let us absorb you. You can learn temperance
In a more temperate climate." Give us just a few decades
Of grace, to encourage the fine art of acquiescence
And we might save the race. Meanwhile, observe our
    creative chaos,
Flux, efflorescence—whatever you care to call it!

Two

I take as my theme, "The Independent Woman,"
Independent but maimed: observe the exigent neckties
Choking violet writers; the sad slacks of stipple-face
    matrons;
Indigo intellectuals, crop-haired and callous-toed,
Cute spectacles, chewed cuticles, aced out by full-tim
    beauties
In the race for a male. Retreating to drabness, bad manner
And sleeping with manuscripts. Forgive our transgression
Of old gallantries as we hitch in chairs, light our ow
    cigarettes,
Not expecting your care, having forfeited it by trying t
    get even.

But we need dependency, cosseting and well-treatment.
So do men sometimes. Why don't they admit it?
We will be cows for a while, because babies howl for u
Be kittens or bitches, who want to eat grass now and the
For the sake of our health. But the role of pastoral heroin
Is not permanent, Jack. We want to get back to th
    meeting.

Knitting booties and brows, tartars or termagants, ancie
Fertility symbols, chained to our cycle, released
Only in part by devices of hygiene and personal daintine
Strapped into our girdles, held down, yet uplifted by mar
Ingenious constructions, holding coiffures in a breeze,
Hobbled and swathed in whimsy, tripping on feminine
Shoes with fool heels, losing our lipsticks, you, me,
In ephemeral stockings, clutching our handbags a
    packages.

Our masks, always in peril of smearing or cracking,
In need of continuous check in the mirror or silverware
Keep us in thrall to ourselves, concerned with our surfac
Look at man's uniform drabness, his impersonal envelop

Over chicken wrists or meek shoulders, a formal, hard-
  fibered assurance.
The drape of the male is designed to achieve self-forget-
  fulness.

So, sister, forget yourself a few times and see where it gets
  you:
Up the creek, alone with your talent, sans everything else.
You can wait for the menopause, and catch up on your
  reading.
So primp, preen, prink, pluck and prize your flesh,
All posturings! All ravishment! All sensibility!
Meanwhile, have you used your mind today?
What pomegranate raised you from the dead,
Springing, full-grown, from your own head, Athena?

Three

I will speak about women of letters, for I'm in the racket.
Our biggest successes to date? Old maids to a woman.
And our saddest conspicuous failures? The married
  spinsters
On loan to the husbands they treated like surrogate fathers.
Think of that crew of self-pitiers, not-very-distant,
Who carried the torch for themselves and got first-degree
  burns.
Or the sad sonneteers, toast-and-teasdales we loved at
  thirteen;
Middle-aged virgins seducing the puerile anthologists.
Through lust-of-the-mind; barbiturate-drenched Camilles
With continuous periods, murmuring softly on sofas
When poetry wasn't a craft but a sickly effluvium,
The air thick with incense, musk, and emotional blackmail.

I suppose they reacted from an earlier womanly modesty
When too many girls were scabs to their stricken sisterhood,
Impugning our sex to stay in good with the men,
Commencing their insecure bluster. How they must have
  swaggered

When women themselves indorsed their own inferiority
Vestals, vassals and vessels, rolled into several,
They took notes in rolling syllabics, in careful journals,
Aiming to please a posterity that despises them.
But we'll always have traitors who swear that a woman
    surrenders
Her Supreme Function, by equating Art with aggression
And failure with Femininity. Still, it's just as unfair
To equate Art with Femininity, like a prettily-packaged
    commodity
When we are the custodians of the world's best-kept secret
Merely the private lives of one-half of humanity.

But even with masculine dominance, we mares and
    mistresses
Produced some sleek saboteuses, making their cracks
Which the porridge-brained males of the day were too
    thick to perceive,
Mistaking young hornets for perfectly harmless bumble
    bees.
Being thought innocuous rouses some women to frenzy;
They try to be ugly by aping the ways of the men
And succeed. Swearing, sucking cigars and scorching the
    bedspread,
Slopping straight shots, eyes blotted, vanity-blown
In the expectation of glory: *she writes like a man!*
This drives other women mad in a mist of chiffon
(one poetess draped her gauze over red flannels, a practical
    feminist).

But we're emerging from all that, more or less,
Except for some lady-like laggards and Quarterly priest
    esses
Who flog men for fun, and kick women to maim competi
    tion.
Now, if we struggle abnormally, we may almost seem
    normal;
If we submerge our self-pity in disciplined industry;
If we stand up and be hated, and swear not to sleep with
    editors;

f we regard ourselves formally, respecting our true
   limitations
Without making an unseemly show of trying to unfreeze
   our assets;
Keeping our heads and our pride while remaining un-
   married;
And if wedded, kill guilt in its tracks when we stack up the
   dishes
And defect to the typewriter. And if mothers, believe in the
   luck of our children,
Whom we forbid to devour us, whom we shall not devour,
And the luck of our husbands and lovers, who keep free
   women.

THE INTRUDER

My mother—preferring the strange to the tame:
Dove-note, bone marrow, deer dung,
Frog's belly distended with finny young,
Leaf-mould wilderness, hare-bell, toadstool,
Odd, small snakes roving through the leaves,
Metallic beetles rambling over stones: all
Wild and natural!—flashed out her instinctive love, and
   quick, she
Picked up the fluttering, bleeding bat the cat laid at her
   feet,
And held the little horror to the mirror, where
He gazed on himself, and shrieked like an old screen door
   far off.

Depended from her pinched thumb, each wing
Came clattering down like a small black shutter.
Still tranquil, she began, "It's rather sweet. . . ."
The soft mouse body, the hard feral glint
In the caught eyes. Then we saw,
And recoiled: lice, pallid, yellow,
Nested within the wing-pits, cosily sucked and snoozed.
The thing dropped from her hands, and with its thud,

Swiftly, the cat, with a clean careful mouth
Closed on the soiled webs, growling, took them out to th
    back stoop.

But still, dark blood, a sticky puddle on the floor
Remained, of all my mother's tender, wounding passion
For a whole wild, lost, betrayed and secret life
Among its dens and burrows, its clean stones,
Whose denizens can turn upon the world
With spitting tongue, an odor, talon, claw,
To sting or soil benevolence, alien
As our clumsy traps, our random scatter of shot.
She swept to the kitchen. Turning on the tap,
She washed and washed the pity from her hands.

LEATRICE W. EMERUWA, a native of Cleveland, Ohio, holds degrees from Howard and Kent State Universities and has done additional graduate work at New York and Case Western Universities. She is currently an Assistant Professor at the Metropolitan Campus of Cuyahoga Community College and specializes in Black literature and creative writing. She also advises two student literary magazines as well as the New World Arts Workshop. Her play *Black Magic Anyone?* was produced by the Cuyahoga Community College's Experimental One World Theatre Workshop in the summer of 1971. She has recently published a small book of poems, and has three volumes, *Black Venus in Gemini; Black Girl, Black Girl;* and *Rap-time in Rhythm,* ready for publication.

153

MAKING OUT

The Widow
met a big blk
bad-mouthing-charley cat
t'other day.   But like "hey!"
that revolutionary came on with
this un-Malcolm-like
nigger crap.   Like "say":

"You blk sister now
bes in style. Right on!

Git wit it.   Groove. Lemme
Rip off sum.
Better lay it on me strong, babe-ee
while you got the chance.
Who knows how long this
dark-meat-bag'll last."

The Widow
Jest smiled.   Fighting tuh
keep her afro cool.   Batted
dark Euphration eyes.   Cooed:
(tho madder 'n hell/burning fire inside)
"Long-lean-daddy-o, I got news
for You.   Dig!
I mo do you a bad blk boo-ga-loo
Cause even chuckie knows
how that ole saying goes:
"The blker the berry, the sweeter the juice."
You know what I mean
Dig on it!"

"PERSONALS"

*(Newspaper "personal" items: "Sadie, the
cleaning woman, please call Mrs. Blake.")*

Sadie
the cleaning lady:
"I ain't stud'n her
cause I dun got
tired from my nose
to my toes of
Miz Blake (alias Miz Ann)
messing aroun' to make
one month's dirt be a day!!"

JEANETTE NICHOLS was born and raised in New Haven, Connecticut. She studied to be a painter but turned instead to writing. In 1959 she was invited to the Bread Loaf Writers' Conference as a Scholar, being among the first ten young writers to be extended this honor. She lives in East Haven and works for Yale University. Her books of poems include *Mostly People* (1966) and *Emblems of Passage* (1968).

A KIND OF LOVE

for Michael O'Malley

He wanted to pat
the bellies of pregnant women
and say "well done, well done."
Passing on sidewalks,
hands in pockets, head down,
for the moment that love takes
he loved them,
whispering to each one
like a Father or lover, "good girl, good girl."

SOMEONE GONE AWAY DOWNSTAIRS

He has been washed and locked in
for the night
and the dark outside
is coming down heavy. He could
sleep except for the teacups
chattering upstairs,
except for the darkness
and the coming down
hard. So he sits on the bed
which is his bed and chews
on a peeled sliver of wood
from its headboard. His head
lolls onto one shoulder which moves
as he chews, as the veins in his
temples move. Upstairs talk runs
as normal as water. No one asks
for the little monster of the cellar.
He has been away forever. Later
as the heavy dark lifts

she will come bringing sleep
calling him Sweet Melon
and place his head straight
on the pillow again.

MY FATHER
TOURED THE SOUTH

My father and his muscles
toured the South posing
in store windows stripped down
past his biceps. He was young then,
dark eyes like dates, hair
like a black sandbar. Full of rush
to crush cities and worlds
like the air he shushed off
when he brought the loose strap up
round his chest and inhaled
till he filled it, proving
the power of physical culture.

When I was nine and he in the forties
I found his pictures, profiled in tights
like a small John L. He laughed
when I showed them, and with a thumb
in his mouth blew up his arm
like an auto tire we tried
to squeeze down and couldn't.

Now that proud and laughing strength
folds to a memory of store windows
and caught ohs from his children's lips
as he hefted us up to the ceiling
and swung us back like easy dumbbells.
His arms are half-caste traitors to a wish
with no more weights to lift,
nothing his youth need move by muscle,

no cities to push flat for the sake
of proving strength. Only the muscles in his head
still flex and dance as his arms did once
in that old thumb game and the strap
across his brain pulls tight again and again.

THE SAME LADY

I

I hear April's shudder of gutter lakes,
limbering roots and mud flowing
slick and rich as gravy
in rutted dirt roads, bubbling
along corner lawns walked bare
and seething between the untarred
city slots where the earth leaks
over macadam and cement:
April's ooze and worked-up sweat
making a job of the season.
And I reason that mud
is a sweet old girl's ageless
glands gone wild again for love,
a girl blown lilac-windy and
risen to her sweet numb knees.

II

Fat old lady Spring again.
No sylph-like girl this
bud waddle, green swaddling
and full-grown winds
warning: "Appreciate". We
return to that old juice
hoping to stay loose, stay
loose. But few of us impervious
to May can stand the stake of roses
in the heart, and not go gay,

go adolescent and roundelay,
roundelay. Voom go the pom pom
buds and grasses, slurp goes the sap;
and the pap of the world lifts up, up
to these old humdrum lips; and fe, fo,
fi, fum, this beanstalk giant
tumbles head over shin into
the sweet obesity of Spring.

Jed Fielding

MAXINE KUMIN was born in 1925 and now lives in Newton Highlands, Massachusetts, with her husband and three children. She received her B.A. and M.A. from Radcliffe College, and has been Instructor of English at Tufts University, a consultant in literature to the Central Atlantic Regional Educational Laboratory, and consultant to the Board of Coordinated Educational Services. She now teaches a seminar in creative writing at Newton College of the Sacred Heart. She has received several poetry awards, including a grant from the National Council on the Arts and the Humanities. Her books of poetry include *The Nightmare Factory, The Privilege,* and *Halfway.* She has also written children's books and three novels, *Through Dooms of Love, The Passions of Uxport,* and *The Abduction.*

MOTHER ROSARINE

Next-door Mother Rosarine
of the square white front and black buckram
tugged up the morning with cinches of keys,
rode through The Mass, a bristle-chinned queen,
jingling the tongues that unlocked the linens,
the larder, the gym suits that luffed at the knees
of the boarders, and swung on the door to His Kingdom

through which I did not dare pass.
I came in screw curls and dotted swisses,
came through the hedge to that swaddled lap.
Cheeks on her starch, a traitor to my class,
I nibbled Christ's toes on the rosewood cross
and begged her, Mother, take off your cap.
Oh I filled up my vestal with baby kisses.

Wrong, born wrong for the convent games
I hunched on the sidelines, beggar fashion.
My child, said Mother Rosarine,
rooting for your side is a useful passion.
She led three cheers and a locomotive for the team.
Beet-red Sister Mary Claire, a victim
of rashes, refereed. She called for time.

At vespers, hot in my body still,
I stole back in up the convent stairs
and sat alone with the varnished smell
of the scribbled desks, and dreamed of angels.
There were lids to pry in that chalkdust air.
A rosary strung with lacquer-black kernels
slid in my pocket. It polished my fingers.

The seeds grew wet in my palm. Going down,
clicking the blessings I made my own
and testing the treads for creaks, I could hear

other Rosarine's voice turn the churn downstairs.
the buttery sunset, in the beadroll mansion,
r nuns, like rows of cows in their stanchions
tly mooing, were making the sound of prayer.

AFTER LOVE

Afterwards, the compromise.
Bodies resume their boundaries.

These legs, for instance, mine.
Your arms take you back in.

Spoons of our fingers, lips
admit their ownership.

The bedding yawns, a door
blows aimlessly ajar

and overhead, a plane
singsongs coming down.

Nothing is changed, except
there was a moment when

the wolf, the mongering wolf
who stands outside the self

lay lightly down, and slept.

Bernice B. Perry

CAROLYN STOLOFF was born in New York City. She received a B.S. degree in painting from Columbia University. Her paintings and drawings have been in many shows across the country. Her poems have appeared in over forty publications, and her first book of poems, *Stepping Out,* was published by the Unicorn Press in 1971. She has received the Theodore Roethke Award from *Poetry Northwest* and a large grant from the National Council on the Arts. She teaches painting, drawing, and creative writing at Manhattanville College, New York.

OPPOSITES

What could we do, he and I:
the Norseman who didn't discover America,
and I, candy-striped from a Turkish Bazaar?
What would we do together?
I, a lithe coconut palm nodding by an oasis,
he, a huntsman trudging
up to his waist in snow.
How could he catch me,
his line baited with minnows
to tempt a dolphin from the dense sea?
What call could he utter
through those linear lips
that would move my lusty hull
to rock him safely on night waters?
How could the same house hold us?
me with my frozen fingers,
him with his mango desire.

SHORT SUBJECTS

homage to Magritte

I. TO CATCH A CLOUD

begin with an unruffled lake
wait for a cloud to pass over
see the cloud in the lake
reach down   pinch the lake's
skin between thumb and forefinger
raise it as you would a silk
handkerchief   the cloud will stick
put it in your pocket

II. SOUVENIR

begin with the Yangtze
you are on it watching sampans
an orange sunset
stand   without rocking the boat
reach as high as you can
grip a corner in each hand
and peel down to your feet

write a message on the back
stamp and mail

III. LOGIC

begin with a feather picked up
on a walk in Vermont or Central Park
glue it to paper
draw a bird around it

claim your bird has flown

IV. RETRIBUTION I

begin with an empty cup
take it by the ear and shake it
turn it upside down on the saucer
knock on the bottom with a spoon
when you hear a hiss
lift the lid and let one escape

keep the others as hostages

V. RETRIBUTION II

paint an elephant on a plain
a few miles away

with tweezers transfer
to your enemy's ear

FOR THE SUICIDE'S DAUGHTER

In the narrow

> closet under the stairs, its curved
> claws retracted in ferocious fur, the bear
> slept long after they found her curled
> on the tiled floor, as in the parlor

grave

> and correct relatives revolved
> among the stuffed chairs murmuring:
> *Dreadful accident. Shocking thing*
> *to happen. Poor child;* but you,

the child

> who had laughed in the circus of her skirts,
> caught the smell of the broom closet
> in the empty glass she left,
> though they rinsed it well, and

sat

> choked but defiant. *Cat*
> *got your tongue?* You were sure. *Say*
> *PLEASE*
> *and it's yours.* You knew, but you couldn't
> say it so you screwed up your face,

tasting

> the clean bite of silence. *Watch out!*
> warned the aunts and cousins, *it will freeze*
> *that way.* They wondered if the tight cords
> would bend, as they stood between you and
the ritual of naming.

> At bedtime, sweat formed
> on your child's palm, still creased
> with wisdom from the wet, as you crept
> up the steps, cautious.

One night,

> deep in your dilations, the winter tongue
>   awoke.
> *Bear!* you called. *Bear, BARE,* at the door.
> *Lye. Lye, LIARS,* you screamed
> as the glass broke.

Older

>you stamped as you climbed to the man
>who came to board up the closet, to strum
>as you clapped in your tall
>mother's shadow, rapped

in the skin

>of her heat and color, as you
>tapped with your heels: *Look! there is no
>hell or punishment, no hollow
>place under this land.*

You spoke,

>bare in the night room, with intense
>gestures: *No furs for me,
>or ribbons either.* Instead, retrievers,
>named, responsive, and through the dark

a girl

>feels her way freely to find her
>doors to open. In the kennel
>dogs bark. Between their paws rest
>the bones of cold dancers.

BEARING IT

Metsovon, Greece 196*

>Bodies lift burdens
>sacked   to shoulders   to backs
>carry wool to spin
>twigs to burn   grain
>water in earthen jugs
>baked hollows for bearing   men
>lift blocks of bone
>building shells for shelter
>holes to lie down in
>to be warmed by women   wormed
>into by infants   men love
>marry   carry stones
>and wooden bones   curved

roof tiles   raise
place   secure
these with mortar
women bend at fountains
catching flow in hollows
rise with transparent water
weight on shoulders   in breasts
bellies   men leave
staffs in hand   tear
down   batter   break
scatter what holds
ravish what's held   make
over   fill women's
baskets and bowls with fish
loaves   men
leave   come home again

Rollie McKenna

ANNE SEXTON was born in Newton, Massachusetts in 1928. She married in 1948, and had two daughters. She attended Garland Junior College, Boston Adult Center for Education, Boston University, and Brandeis University. She started writing in 1957, held the Robert Frost Fellowship in 1960 at Bread Loaf Writers' Conference, and was a scholar at Radcliffe Institute for Independent Study from 1961 to 1963, teaching creative writing at Harvard and Radcliffe during 1961. She received several traveling grants and awards, including the Pulitzer Prize for Poetry in 1967 for *Live or Die*. Houghton Mifflin has published *To Bedlam and Part Way Back* (1960), *All My Pretty Ones* (1962), *Live or Die* (1966), *Love Poems* (1969), and *Transformations* (1971). Oxford University Press has published *Selected Poems*. Her play *Mercy Street* was the first production of the American Place Theatre in New York in 1969. She died, a probable suicide, in 1974.

LITTLE GIRL, MY STRING BEAN,
MY LOVELY WOMAN

My daughter, at eleven
(almost twelve), is like a garden.

Oh, darling! Born in that sweet birthday suit
and having owned it and known it for so long,
now you must watch high noon enter—
noon, that ghost hour.
Oh, funny little girl—this one under a blueberry sky,
this one! How can I say that I've known
just what you know and just where you are?

It's not a strange place, this odd home
where your face sits in my hand
so full of distance,
so full of its immediate fever.
The summer has seized you,
as when, last month in Amalfi, I saw
lemons as large as your desk-side globe—
that miniature map of the world—
and I could mention, too,
the market stalls of mushrooms
and garlic buds all engorged.
Or I think even of the orchard next door,
where the berries are done
and the apples are beginning to swell.
And once, with our first backyard,
I remember I planted an acre of yellow beans
we couldn't eat.

Oh, little girl,
my stringbean,
how do you grow?
You grow this way.
You are too many to eat.

I hear
as in a dream
the conversation of the old wives
speaking of *womanhood.*
I remember that I heard nothing myself.
I was alone.
I waited like a target.

Let high noon enter—
the hour of the ghosts.
Once the Romans believed
that noon was the ghost hour,
and I can believe it, too,
under that startling sun,
and someday they will come to you,
someday, men bare to the waist, young Romans
at noon where they belong,
with ladders and hammers
while no one sleeps.

But before they enter
I will have said,
Your bones are lovely,
and before their strange hands
there was always this hand that formed.

Oh, darling, let your body in,
let it tie you in,
in comfort.
What I want to say, Linda,
is that women are born twice.
If I could have watched you grow
as a magical mother might,
if I could have seen through my magical transparent belly
there would have been such ripening within:
your embryo,
the seed taking on its own,
life clapping the bedpost,

bones from the pond,
thumbs and two mysterious eyes,
the awfully human head,
the heart jumping like a puppy,
the important lungs,
the becoming—
while it becomes!
as it does now,
a world of its own,
a delicate place.

say hello
to such shakes and knockings and high jinks,
such music, such sprouts,
such dancing-mad-bears of music,
such necessary sugar,
such goings-on!

Oh, little girl,
my stringbean,
how do you grow?
You grow this way.
You are too many to eat.

What I want to say, Linda,
is that there is nothing in your body that lies.
All that is new is telling the truth.
I'm here, that somebody else,
an old tree in the background.

Darling,
stand still at your door,
sure of yourself, a white stone, a good stone—
as exceptional as laughter
you will strike fire,
that new thing!

July 14, 1964

RAPUNZEL

A woman
who loves a woman
is forever young.
The mentor
and the student
feed off each other.
Many a girl
had an old aunt
who locked her in the study
to keep the boys away.
They would play rummy
or lie on the couch
and touch and touch.
Old breast against young breast . . .

Let your dress fall down your shoulder,
come touch a copy of you
for I am at the mercy of rain,
for I have left the three Christs of Ypsilanti,
for I have left the long naps of Ann Arbor
and the church spires have turned to stumps.
The sea bangs into my cloister
for the young politicians are dying,
are dying so hold me, my young dear,
hold me . . .

The yellow rose will turn to cinder
and New York City will fall in
before we are done so hold me,
my young dear, hold me.
Put your pale arms around my neck.
Let me hold your heart like a flower
lest it bloom and collapse.
Give me your skin
as sheer as a cobweb,
let me open it up
and listen in and scoop out the dark.

Give me your nether lips
all puffy with their art
and I will give you angel fire in return.
We are two clouds
glistening in the bottle glass.
We are two birds
washing in the same mirror.
We were fair game
but we have kept out of the cesspool.
We are strong.
We are the good ones.
Do not discover us
for we lie together all in green
like pond weeds.
Hold me, my young dear, hold me.

They touch their delicate watches
one at a time.
They dance to the lute
two at a time.
They are as tender as bog moss.
They play mother-me-do
all day.
A woman
who loves a woman
is forever young.

Once there was a witch's garden
more beautiful than Eve's
with carrots growing like little fish,
with many tomatoes rich as frogs,
onions as ingrown as hearts,
the squash singing like a dolphin
and one patch given over wholly to magic—
rampion, a kind of salad root,
a kind of harebell more potent than penicillin,
growing leaf by leaf, skin by skin,
as rapt and as fluid as Isadora Duncan.
However the witch's garden was kept locked
and each day a woman who was with child

looked upon the rampion wildly,
fancying that she would die
if she could not have it.
Her husband feared for her welfare
and thus climbed into the garden
to fetch the life-giving tubers.

Ah ha, cried the witch,
whose proper name was Mother Gothel,
you are a thief and now you will die.
However they made a trade,
typical enough in those times.
He promised his child to Mother Gothel
so of course when it was born
she took the child away with her.
She gave the child the name Rapunzel,
another name for the life-giving rampion.
Because Rapunzel was a beautiful girl
Mother Gothel treasured her beyond all things.
As she grew older Mother Gothel thought:
None but I will ever see her or touch her.
She locked her in a tower without a door
or a staircase. It had only a high window.
When the witch wanted to enter she cried:
Rapunzel, Rapunzel, let down your hair.
Rapunzel's hair fell to the ground like a rainbow.
It was as yellow as a dandelion
and as strong as a dog leash.
Hand over hand she shinnied up
the hair like a sailor
and there in the stone-cold room,
as cold as a museum,
Mother Gothel cried:
Hold me, my young dear, hold me,
and thus they played mother-me-do.

Years later a prince came by
and heard Rapunzel singing in her loneliness.
That song pierced his heart like a valentine
but he could find no way to get to her.

Like a chameleon he hid himself among the trees
and watched the witch ascend the swinging hair.
The next day he himself called out:
Rapunzel, Rapunzel, let down your hair,
and thus they met and he declared his love.
What is this beast, she thought,
with muscles on his arms
like a bag of snakes?
What is this moss on his legs?
What prickly plant grows on his cheeks?
What is this voice as deep as a dog?
Yet he dazzled her with his answers.
Yet he dazzled her with his dancing stick.
They lay together upon the yellowy threads,
swimming through them
like minnows through kelp
and they sang out benedictions like the Pope.

Each day he brought her a skein of silk
to fashion a ladder so they could both escape.
But Mother Gothel discovered the plot
and cut off Rapunzel's hair to her ears
and took her into the forest to repent.
When the prince came the witch fastened
the hair to a hook and let it down.
When he saw that Rapunzel had been banished
he flung himself out of the tower, a side of beef.
He was blinded by thorns that pricked him like tacks.
As blind as Oedipus he wandered for years
until he heard a song that pierced his heart
like that long-ago valentine.
As he kissed Rapunzel her tears fell on his eyes
and in the manner of such cure-alls
his sight was suddenly restored.

They lived happily as you might expect
proving that mother-me-do
can be outgrown,
just as the fish on Friday,
just as a tricycle.

The world, some say,
is made up of couples.
A rose must have a stem.

As for Mother Gothel,
her heart shrank to the size of a pin,
never again to say: Hold me, my young dear,
hold me,
and only as she dreamt of the yellow hair
did moonlight sift into her mouth.

IN CELEBRATION OF MY UTERUS

Everyone in me is a bird.
I am beating all my wings.
They wanted to cut you out
but they will not.
They said you were immeasurably empty
but you are not.
They said you were sick unto dying
but they were wrong.
You are singing like a school girl.
You are not torn.

Sweet weight,
in celebration of the woman I am
and of the soul of the woman I am
and of the central creature and its delight
I sing for you. I dare to live.
Hello, spirit. Hello, cup.
Fasten, cover. Cover that does contain.
Hello to the soil of the fields.
Welcome, roots.

Each cell has a life.
There is enough here to please a nation.
It is enough that the populace own these goods.
Any person, any commonwealth would say of it,

"It is good this year that we may plant again
and think forward to a harvest.
A blight had been forecast and has been cast out."
Many women are singing together of this:
one is in a shoe factory cursing the machine,
one is at the aquarium tending a seal,
one is dull at the wheel of her Ford,
one is at the toll gate collecting,
one is tying the cord of a calf in Arizona,
one is straddling a cello in Russia,
one is shifting pots on the stove in Egypt,
one is painting her bedroom walls moon color,
one is dying but remembering a breakfast,
one is stretching on her mat in Thailand,
one is wiping the ass of her child,
one is staring out the window of a train
in the middle of Wyoming and one is
anywhere and some are everywhere and all
seem to be singing, although some can not
sing a note.

Sweet weight,
in celebration of the woman I am
let me carry a ten-foot scarf,
let me drum for the nineteen-year-olds,
let me carry bowls for the offering
(if that is my part).
Let me study the cardiovascular tissue,
let me examine the angular distance of meteors,
let me suck on the stems of flowers
(if that is my part).
Let me make certain tribal figures
(if that is my part).
For this thing the body needs
let me sing
for the supper,
for the kissing,
for the correct
yes.

CHRISTMAS EVE

Oh sharp diamond my mother!
I could not count the cost
of all your faces, your moods—
that present that I lost.
Sweet girl, my deathbed,
my jewel-fingered lady,
your portrait flickered all night
by the bulbs of the tree.

Your face as calm as the moon
over a mannered sea,
presided at the family reunion,
the twelve grandchildren
you used to wear on your wrist,
a three-months-old baby,
a fat check you never wrote,
the red-haired toddler who danced the twist,
your aging daughters, each one a wife,
each one talking to the family cook,
each one avoiding the portrait,
each one aping your life.

Later, after the party,
after the house went to bed,
I sat up drinking the Christmas brandy,
watching your picture,
letting the tree move in and out of focus.
The bulbs vibrated.
They were a halo over your forehead.
Then they were a beehive,
blue, yellow, green, red;
each one its own juice, each hot and alive
stinging your face. But you did not move.
I continued to watch, forcing myself,
waiting, inexhaustible, thirty-five.

I wanted your eyes, like the shadows
of two small birds, to change.
But they did not age.
The smile that gathered me in, all wit,
all charm, was invincible.
Hour after hour I looked at your face
but I could not pull the roots out of it.
Then I watched how the sun hit
your red sweater, your withered neck,
your badly painted flesh-pink skin.
You who led me by the nose,
I saw you as you were.
Then I thought of your body
as one thinks of murder . . .

Then I said Mary—
Mary, Mary, forgive me
and then I touched a present for the child,
the last I bred before your death;
and then I touched my breast
and then I touched the floor
and then my breast again as if,
somehow, it were one of yours.

FOR MY LOVER,
RETURNING TO HIS WIFE

She is all there.
She was melted carefully down for you
and cast up from your childhood,
cast up from your one hundred favorite aggies.

She has always been there, my darling.
She is, in fact, exquisite.
Fireworks in the dull middle of February
and as real as a cast-iron pot.

Let's face it, I have been momentary.
A luxury. A bright red sloop in the harbor.

My hair rising like smoke from the car window.
Littleneck clams out of season.

She is more than that. She is your have to have,
has grown you your practical your tropical growth.
This is not an experiment. She is all harmony.
She sees to oars and oarlocks for the dinghy,

has placed wild flowers at the window at breakfast,
sat by the potter's wheel at midday,
set forth three children under the moon,
three cherubs drawn by Michelangelo,

done this with her legs spread out
in the terrible months in the chapel.
If you glance up, the children are there
like delicate balloons resting on the ceiling.

She has also carried each one down the hall
after supper, their heads privately bent,
two legs protesting, person to person,
her face flushed with a song and their little sleep.

I give you back your heart.
I give you permission—

for the fuse inside her, throbbing
angrily in the dirt, for the bitch in her
and the burying of her wound—
for the burying of her small red wound alive—

for the pale flickering flare under her ribs,
for the drunken sailor who waits in her left pulse,
for the mother's knee, for the stockings,
for the garter belt, for the call—

the curious call
when you will burrow in arms and breasts
and tug at the orange ribbon in her hair
and answer the call, the curious call.

She is so naked and singular.
She is the sum of yourself and your dream.
Climb her like a monument, step after step.
She is solid.

As for me, I am a watercolor.
I wash off.

RUTH LISA SCHECHTER was born in 1928. She is a native of Boston, but she now lives in New York City. She is the author of *Movable Parts, Suddenly Thunder, Ballet of the Coco Rose,* and *Near the Wall of Lion Shadows.* Her work appeared in the Doubleday anthology, *The Writing on the Wall.* She has been poet-in-residence at Mundelein College, Chicago, and she was granted fellowships at the Mac-Dowell Colony in 1963 and 1970. Her poems have been choreographed throughout the U.S., Canada, and Israel, and her two-act play, *Alan, Carlos, Theresa,* appeared off-off Broadway. She works on the staff of the New York rehabilitation drug agency and at Odyssey House as a Poetry Therapist.

"TERRE DES HOMMES"

We shall have to force ourselves
to remember. This is not juvenile
fiction. In a cold sky
far from where flags wave
children travel
in jet planes. Children
whom no-one will meet to kiss
travel with paper bags over
their heads. Not exactly games. They know
they must not show
what accidents of war remove. From towns of
no face saved. 1960. The Algerian
war. Today
the Vietnamese. It is not enough
to drop attention and regret. We go on
thinking but adjust ways and days
to such details. While I.Q. numbers rise
children go down to the count in
grown-up quarrels that skin them
alive. They are going to England for
Christmas, wrapped in plastic surgery, cotton
and gauze, going to get their faces
back. Beds stay. Reserved in village
hospitals and other places. Now
Cantho, Mytho and Rach Gia. The immense
distress. In Saigon
Jaguars fly
close to gutters where death
will not stop or die. In shock, the embryo
slips from the womb, slips in themes of
madness where nobody has mercy. Cradles
topple. O' we shall be forced
to remember such things.

WHAT IS THERE?

Saturdays
I am telling Anne
there is
a world of Roethke, the rocky
path of poets tapping
keys in the verbal music
that plays for real.

She begins to hear
and recovery is
a new poem
in my hand from Anne
about a picture on her wall
lopsided once
like a suicide note
opening now to read
only Spring.

Recovery
with its quiet
way, with its upset face is
all over the place
shocked in postures, falling
apart, trying balance, pointing
toes, learning to let
darkness go, at times
forgetting why they came
sucked in
by old betrayals.

Who are these people
holding on
to Carol who now
brings cake she baked
while Margaret shrieks:
         "It might be poisoned, who knows
         we can trust her?"

And no-one laughs and no-one cries
as they pull, slow, slow
face to face in the long mirror
of themselves, floating in
hostile air to find out
what is there.

Alfred Adler Mental Hygiene Clinic,
1968

AND WE ARE STRANGERS
TO EACH OTHER

Alone in ourselves.   At midnight
in a gallery of sleep, they come
drifting down to us.   All
those faces

imprisoned
like bronze figures on a base, clubbed
by their own situation, each
with dreams apart.   Lined up in
riddles of catastrophe, hospital
clinics go noisy with genetic
questions.   The sick appear, enamelled
in space

etherized and vague
in experiments that shake us from head
to foot.   And memory records one single
voice, one posture that moves
on.   In a pageant of unknown
causes, a thousand names register
old scar tissue to cross-
stitch our hearts

in dark events
of mysterious gauze.   Mothers

brood where blue-lipped children
stare, profiles in chalk.   Arterial blood
overflows.   Machinery sounds
roar.   The computer cannot process
tears.   Terror finds its own
vocabulary

and no indulgent feelings file
alphabetically.   The lyrical language of
disease trips over family trees
trapped in some powerful
reality.   While people bend, tired
tricked by birth, machines
replace

parts of hope in clocks
set neither right nor wrong for
baby-no-name, bared in stuttering
breath, the fighting for life
that is no dream.   At midnight
in a gallery of sleep.   All
those faces.

The Children's Cardiac Clin
of Montefiore Hospita
New York City, 196

Thomas Victor, for the *New York Quarterly*

ADRIENNE RICH was born in Baltimore, Maryland in 1929. She graduated from Radcliffe College in 1951, and that year her first book of poems, *A Change of World,* was published in the Yale Younger Poets Series. She received a Guggenheim Fellowship which she used to travel in Europe, 1952–1953. She lived in Cambridge, Massachusetts for thirteen years, trying to write and think her way through the "woman-writer-wife-mother tangle." She then spent fifteen months in Holland, learning Dutch and translating Dutch poetry. In 1966 she moved to New York City and taught poetry workshops at Swarthmore College and Columbia University, and then she began teaching in the SEEK program at City College of New York. Her other books of poems include *The Diamond Cutters* (1955), *Snapshots of a Daughter-in-Law* (1962), *Necessities of Life* (1966), *Leaflets* (1969) and *The Will to Change* (1971), all published by W. W. Norton.

LIVING IN SIN

She had thought the studio would keep itself;
no dust upon the furniture of love.
Half heresy, to wish the taps less vocal,
the panes relieved of grime. A plate of pears,
a piano with a Persian shawl, a cat
stalking the picturesque amusing mouse
had risen at his urging.
Not that at five each separate stair would writhe
under the milkman's tramp; that morning light
so coldly would delineate the scraps
of last night's cheese and three sepulchral bottles;
that on the kitchen shelf among the saucers
a pair of beetle-eyes would fix her own—
envoy from some black village in the mouldings . . .
Meanwhile, he, with a yawn,
sounded a dozen notes upon the keyboard,
declared it out of tune, shrugged at the mirror,
rubbed at his beard, went out for cigarettes;
while she, jeered by the minor demons,
pulled back the sheets and made the bed and found
a towel to dust the table-top,
and let the coffee-pot boil over on the stove.
By evening she was back in love again,
though not so wholly but throughout the night
she woke sometimes to feel the daylight coming
like a relentless milkman up the stairs.

THE BOOK

for Richard Howard

You, hiding there in your words
like a disgrace
the cast-off son of a family
whose face is written in theirs

who must not be mentioned
who calls collect three times a year
from obscure towns out-of-state
and whose calls are never accepted
You who had to leave alone
and forgot your shadow hanging under the stairs
let me tell you: I have been in the house
  have spoken to all of them
they will not pronounce your name
they only allude to you
rising and sitting, going or coming,
falling asleep and waking,
giving away in marriage or calling for water
on their deathbeds
their faces look into each other and see
you
when they write at night in their diaries they are writing
to you

1968

PLANETARIUM

*(Thinking of Caroline Herschel, 1750–1848,
astronomer, sister of William; and others)*

A woman in the shape of a monster
a monster in the shape of a woman
the skies are full of them

a woman   'in the snow
among the Clocks and instruments
or measuring the ground with poles'

in her 98 years to discover
  comets

she whom the moon ruled
like us
levitating into the night sky
riding the polished lenses

Galaxies of women, there
doing penance for impetuousness
ribs chilled
in those spaces   of the mind

An eye,
      'virile, precise and absolutely certain'
      from the mad webs of Uranisborg
                        encountering the NOVA

every impulse of light exploding
from the core
as life flies out of us

      Tycho whispering at last
      'Let me not seem to have lived in vain'

What we see, we see
and seeing is changing

the light that shrivels a mountain
and leaves a man alive

Heartbeat of the pulsar
heart sweating through my body

The radio impulse
pouring in from Taurus

      I am bombarded yet   I stand

I have been standing all my life in the
direct path of a battery of signals
the most accurately transmitted most
untranslateable language in the universe

I am a galactic cloud so deep   so invo-
luted that a light wave could take 15
years to travel through me   And has
taken   I am an instrument in the shape
of a woman trying to translate pulsations
into images   for the relief of the body
and the reconstruction of the mind.

1968

TRYING TO TALK WITH A MAN

Out in this desert we are testing bombs.

That's why we came here.

Sometimes I feel an underground river
forcing its way between deformed cliffs
an acute angle of understanding
moving itself like a locus of the sun
into this condemned scenery.

What we've had to give up to get here:
whole lp collections, the films we starred in
playing in the neighborhoods, bakery windows
full of dry, chocolate-filled Jewish cookies,
the language of love-letters, of suicide notes,
afternoons on the riverbank
pretending to be children

Coming out
to this desert we meant to change the face of
camping among dull-green succulents
walking at noon in the ghost-town
surrounded by a silence

that sounds like the silence of the place
except that it came with us

and is familiar
and everything we were saying until now
was an effort to blot it out
Coming out here we are up against it

Out here I feel more helpless
with you than without you
You mention the danger
and list the equipment
we talk of people caring for each other
in emergencies—laceration, thirst—
but you look at me like an emergency

Your dry heat feels like power
your eyes are stars of a different magnitude
they reflect lights that spell out EXIT
when you get up and pace the floor

talking of the danger
as if it were not ourselves
as if we were testing anything else.

THE MIRROR IN WHICH
TWO ARE SEEN AS ONE

"The situation can be changed only by the patient changing herself. Nothing can be changed in the mother, for she
is dead. And the friend cannot be nagged into changing. If
she wants to change, that is her own affair."   —C. G. Jung

I

She is the one you call sister.
Her simplest act has glamor,
as when she scales a fish the knife
flashes in her long fingers

no motion wasted or when
rapidly talking of love
she steel-wool-burnishes
the battered kettle

Love-apples cramp you sideways
with sudden emptiness
the cereals glutting you, the grains
ripe clusters picked by hand
Love: the refrigerator
with open door
the ripe steaks bleeding
their hearts out in plastic film
the whipped butter, the apricots
the sour leftovers

A crate is waiting in the orchard
for you to fill it
your hands are raw with scraping
the sharp bark, the thorns
of this succulent tree
Pick, pick, pick
this harvest is a failure
the juice runs down your cheekbones
like sweat or tears

2

She is the one you call sister
you blaze like lightning about the room
flicker around her like fire
dazzle yourself in her wide eyes
listing her unfelt needs
thrusting the tenets of your life
into her hands

She moves through a world of India print
her body dappled

with softness, the paisley swells at her hip
walking the street in her cotton shift
buying fresh figs because you love them
photographing the ghetto because you took her there

Why are you crying dry up your tears
we are sisters
words fail you in the stare of her hunger
you hand her another book
scored by your pencil
you hand her a record
of two flutes in India reciting

3

Late summer night the insects
fry in the yellowed lightglobe
your skin burns gold in its light
In this mirror, who are you?   Dreams of the nunnery
with its discipline, the nursery
with its nurse, the hospital
where all the powerful ones are masked
the shop where she thinks the dresses look like you
the graveyard where you sit on the graves
of women who died in childbirth
and women who died at birth

Dreams of your sister's birth
your mother dying in childbirth over and over
not knowing how to stop
bearing you over and over

your mother dead and you unborn
your two hands grasping your head
drawing it down against the blade of life
your nerves the nerves of a midwife
learning her trade

COLETTE INEZ was born in Brussels, Belgium in 1931, and now resides in Orangeburg, New York, with her husband, a free-lance writer. Her first book of poems, *The Woman Who Loved Worms,* was published by Doubleday in 1972. Her work appears in *Quickly Aging Here, Live Poetry* and *Their Place in the Heat.* She was until recently a teacher in the New York City Anti-Poverty Program.

THE WOMAN WHO LOVED WORMS

(from a Japanese legend)

Disdaining butterflies
as frivolous,
she puttered with caterpillars,
and wore a coarse kimono,
crinkled and loose at the neck.

Refused to tweeze her brows
to crescents,
and scowled beneath dark bands
of caterpillar fur.

Even the stationery
on which she scrawled
unkempt calligraphy,
startled the jade-inlaid
indolent ladies,
whom she despised
like the butterflies
wafting kimono sleeves
through senseless poems
about moonsets and peonies;
popular rot of the times.

No, she loved worms,
blackening the moon of her nails
with mud and slugs,
root gnawing grubs,
and the wing case of beetles.

And crouched in the garden,
tugging at her unpinned hair,
weevils queuing across her bare
and unbound feet.

Swift as wasps, the years.
Midge, tick and maggot words
crowded her haikus
and lines on her skin turned her old,
thin as a spinster cricket.

Noon in the snow pavillion,
gulping heated saki,
she recalled Lord Unamuro,
preposterous toad
squatting by the teatray,
proposing with conditions,
a suitable marriage.

Ha!   She stoned imaginary butterflies,
and pinching dirt,
crawled to death's cocoon
dragging a moth to inspect
in the long afternoon.

GOOD NEWS!   NILDA IS BACK

Good news! Nilda is back,
the sign huzzahs
in the Beauty Shoppe

as the rain combs
the sky over and over
like a grandmother combing
the hair of a child.

Impermanent waves
of rain on the street;
the trees are straight
but the city bends.

Nilda is back
from Guayaquil,

Quito, Ponce,
San José

to tease the gringo smiles
of blue-eyed wives
in the raining city.

And now she cha chas up the aisles
to supervise the upswept lines
of an aging lady

who does not know why Nilda comes
or why she goes
or where her hair uncurls at night
damp at the edge from waves of love.

INSTRUCTIONS FOR THE ERECTION
OF A STATUE OF MYSELF
IN CENTRAL PARK

Let me be formed with stone;
a slab of diorite between my ears
will do for brains,
a round cut ruby for a heart.

Breasts? Alabaster mounds
that will not sag from suckling time,
against which birds will bat their wings
and rain will stroke and wind . . .

Cold to sex, and blood, and birth,
drape my marble thighs with snow.
Then let the lovers, hot with quarreling and tears,
stand in my shadow and kiss.

Dr. Marvin E. Neipris

BARBARA GREENBERG was born in 1932. She was "conservatively educated" in the liberal arts, B.A. from Wellesley in 1953, M.A. from Simmons. Her poetry has been published in a number of magazines and anthologies, including *Quickly Aging Here*. She has also written short stories and a play for children. She is married and has two sons.

201

POEM FOR SUSAN

After you dived from the barnacled rocks and swam in the
    shark-stained ocean
you climbed back up to our summer house, your dark hair
    tangled in the sunset,
and told us about the spinster woman, the maiden aunt
    who lives in you.

You said that nothing you are is yours and nothing you do
    consumes you;
that even when you are most in love, most ardent with men
    or women,
the pitiful spinster pulls at your limbs and blushes
    and burns with envy.

And her eyes behind your eyes, you said, are yellow and
    wet with fever
like fishes' eyes, implacably sad, beyond your power
    to close them.
Even your sleep is not your own. She walks on your
    dreams like a spider.

But when you run with the dogs, dance in a red gown
    outsing the choir,
you stir and torment the spinster woman, because she is
    always watching.
And you will have no cut flowers in your house, nor lace
    on your dresses, to spite her.

Even your own dear daughters and sons, who touch your
    hair and embrace you,
are quills in her loveless childless heart. She shivers and
    begs your pardon.
Again you hug your children—again—to feel her wince
    in your being.

This is the photograph we took when you climbed the cliff
    to our cottage:

your features carved by the ocean wind and your hair
    stretched out uncensored
and the spinster woman crouched in the rocks, invisible as
    granite.

THE HUSBAND

He'd never wrung the
neck of a rabbit, a
goose or a sparrow, not
any until
in the night
with a cat
at the back of the cellar
he strangled and strangled.

But why? said his wife
with the chill on her nipples
and fur in her mouth
and the cat eyes staring.
Why did you bring it
why bring it to me?

And the thousands of cats
were the jaws of her question, they
mewed up the night from their
thousands of fences.

He sucked at his tongue and was drunk on the juices.

SURVIVAL

If ever I am an old lady
I want to be an elegant old lady
redolent of pungent essences, like bayberry.

I plan to be lean
with Gothic hands and vein embroidered skin
and prominent eyes that know what most things mean.

My great-granddaughters will be wary
of my eyes, my scent, my strange vocabulary.
I shall serve them tea and wafers while I sip sherry.

I shall make them mine with trinkets:
handkerchiefs and scarabs, wigs and lockets,
skeletons and seashells.   I shall fill their baskets.

Then they will ask me for my story
and I shall tell them—tell a phantom story
frail as candleberry smoke.   Truer than history.

JUST AFTER THE WIDOW'S DEATH

1. The Living Room

Her Chinese lamps
are finished sentences
and her philosophies
are hammered silver snakes with ruby eyeballs.
At her hearth
are once-upon-a-childhood wishes made and granted.

On every wall of this, her ceremonial room,
are clear glass shelves
(like sleeping water or we know not what
pure stratum of her completed self)
where round jewels balance.

Her poet, bound in leather, suffers
no misinterpretation.
Twin porcelain angels in a blush of health
repeat her prayers
and three jade dragons

like contented appetites
forget how fierce their purpose.
On the mantlepiece a crystal bird
sings winter light and consummated loves.

2. The Bedroom

What dime store stylist has . . . ?   That is,
the flapping ruffles, the embarrassments of dust,
the goldfish bubbling in their . . .   No,
not plaster spaniels, not
the hot pink palsy of her . . .   Oh, but yes,
it is.   Her pink, her bed, her flowered wall,
her Saint Cecilia framed in tin, her box
of, in their fluted nests, soft center chocolates
each bitten into . . .

There is no message
scotch-taped to the mirror, reading
Friends, remember . . .
What is, is twisted on the bed:
a wash gray sleepy-doll, its button eyes
torn off, its once-enamelled mouth
a crusty streak, an insolent cry of
want, I want, I want.

LINDA PASTAN was born in New York City in 1932. She received her B.A. from Radcliffe College in 1954 and her M.A. from Brandeis University in 1957. In 1955 she received the Dylan Thomas Poetry Award from *Mademoiselle*. Her poems have appeared in a variety of periodicals, including *The Nation*, *The Saturday Review* and the *Sewanee Review*, and her first book, *A Perfect Circle of Sun*, was published by Swallow Press. She is on the staff of *Voyages*, and lives in Maryland with her husband and three children.

NOTES FROM THE DELIVERY ROOM

Strapped down,
victim in an old comic book,
I have been here before,
this place where pain winces
off the walls
like too bright light.
Bear down a doctor says,
foreman to sweating laborer,
but this work, this forcing
of one life from another
is something that I signed for
at a moment when I would have signed anything.
Babies should grow in fields;
common as beets or turnips
they should be picked and held
root end up, soil spilling
from between their toes—
and how much easier it would be later,
returning them to earth.
Bear up . . . bear down . . . the audience
grows restive, and I'm a new magician
who can't produce the rabbit
from my swollen hat.
She's crowning, someone says,
but there is no one royal here,
just me, quite barefoot,
greeting my barefoot child.

DISTANCES

You travel across the room.
Two chairs and a table
are between us; the shapes
of your words are between us.
Straight and cold as railroad track

I lie in my old roadbed
measuring distances—
waiting for you to pass
over me once again,
on your way somewhere else.

AT THE GYNECOLOGIST'S

The body so carefully
contrived for pain,
wakens from the dream of health
again and again
to hands impersonal as wax
and instruments that pry
into the closed chapters of flesh.
See me here, my naked legs
caught in these metal stirrups,
galloping towards death
with flowers of ether in my hair.

From: WILLIAMSBURG

The Governor's Palace

I am waiting by the canal.
A few violets are scattered near the bench like footnotes
everything else is perfectly green.
Now the cries of children rise from the formal maze,
and the cameras whir and click, persistent
as locusts in the wavy air.
In the governor's palace
the tourists browse like responsible cattle
under a portrait of the governor's wife.
Her face is formal and still.
Around her, slaves lose themselves
in the darkening canvas;

only their eyes show up and their white caps,
like the ghosts of moths who will haunt our screens forever.
Children, come out of the labyrinth,
though the minotaur bears your mother's name
and your father's horns.   You will trip on the fine grass,
cut your delicate hands on the clipped hedges.
Play instead in the kitchen garden.
Discover the bright yams
pulled from the earth, round and bursting as udders,
the black soil still clinging to their roots
like water.
Search out the young peas, already impatient
in their pods.
Learn the new, green taste of raw beans.

SYLVIA PLATH was born in Boston in 1932. She went to Smith College and won the *Mademoiselle* College Fiction Contest. After attending Cambridge University on a Fulbright grant she taught at Smith. She was married to the English poet Ted Hughes and they lived with their two children in Devonshire. She won a number of poetry prizes including *Poetry*'s Bess Hokin Award and the first prize at the Cheltenham Festival in England in 1961. Her books of poetry include, *The Colossus*, Random House, *Ariel*, *Crossing the Water*, and *Winter Trees*, all published by Harper & Row. She committed suicide in 1962 at the age of thirty.

LESBOS

Viciousness in the kitchen!
The potatoes hiss.
It is all Hollywood, windowless,
The fluorescent light wincing on and off like a terrible
      migraine,
Coy paper strips for doors————
Stage curtains, a widow's frizz.
And I, love, am a pathological liar,
And my child—look at her, face down on the floor,
Little unstrung puppet, kicking to disappear————
Why she is schizophrenic,
Her face red and white, a panic,
You have stuck her kittens outside your window
In a sort of cement well
Where they crap and puke and cry and she can't hear.
You say you can't stand her,
The bastard's a girl.
You who have blown your tubes like a bad radio
Clear of voices and history, the staticky
Noise of the new.
You say I should drown the kittens. Their smell!
You say I should drown my girl.
She'll cut her throat at ten if she's mad at two.
The baby smiles, fat snail,
From the polished lozenges of orange linoleum.
You could eat him. He's a boy.
You say your husband is just no good to you.
His Jew-Mama guards his sweet sex like a pearl.
You have one baby, I have two.
I should sit on a rock off Cornwall and comb my hair.
I should wear tiger pants, I should have an affair.
We should meet in another life, we should meet in air,
Me and you.

Meanwhile there's a stink of fat and baby crap.
I'm doped and thick from my last sleeping pill.
The smog of cooking, the smog of hell

Floats our heads, two venomous opposites,
Our bones, our hair.
I call you Orphan, orphan. You are ill.
The sun gives you ulcers, the wind gives you T.B.
Once you were beautiful.
In New York, in Hollywood, the men said: "Through?
Gee baby, you are rare."
You acted, acted, acted for the thrill.
The impotent husband slumps out for a coffee.
I try to keep him in,
An old pole for the lightning,
The acid baths, the skyfuls off of you.
He lumps it down the plastic cobbled hill,
Flogged trolley. The sparks are blue.
The blue sparks spill,
Splitting like quartz into a million bits.

O jewel! O valuable!
That night the moon
Dragged its blood bag, sick
Animal
Up over the harbor lights.
And then grew normal,
Hard and apart and white.
The scale-sheen on the sand scared me to death.
We kept picking up handfuls, loving it,
Working it like dough, a mulatto body,
The silk grits.
A dog picked up your doggy husband. He went on.

Now I am silent, hate
Up to my neck,
Thick, thick.
I do not speak.
I am packing the hard potatoes like good clothes,
I am packing the babies,
I am packing the sick cats.
O vase of acid,
It is love you are full of. You know who you hate.
He is hugging his ball and chain down by the gate

hat opens to the sea
here it drives in, white and black,
hen spews it back.
very day you fill him with soul-stuff, like a pitcher.
ou are so exhausted.
our voice my ear-ring,
apping and sucking, blood-loving bat.
hat is that. That is that.
ou peer from the door,
d hag. "Every woman's a whore.
can't communicate."

see your cute décor
lose on you like the fist of a baby
r an anemone, that sea
weetheart, that kleptomaniac.
am still raw.
say I may be back.
ou know what lies are for.

ven in your Zen heaven we shan't meet.

EDGE

The woman is perfected.
Her dead

Body wears the smile of accomplishment,
The illusion of a Greek necessity

Flows in the scrolls of her toga,
Her bare

Feet seem to be saying:
We have come so far, it is over.

Each dead child coiled, a white serpent,
One at each little

Pitcher of milk, now empty.
She has folded

Them back into her body as petals
Of a rose close when the garden

Stiffens and odours bleed
From the sweet, deep throats of the night flower.

The moon has nothing to be sad about,
Staring from her hood of bone.

She is used to this sort of thing.
Her blacks crackle and drag.

DADDY

You do not do, you do not do
Any more, black shoe
In which I have lived like a foot
For thirty years, poor and white,
Barely daring to breathe or Achoo.

Daddy, I have had to kill you.
You died before I had time——
Marble-heavy, a bag full of God,
Ghastly statue with one grey toe
Big as a Frisco seal

And a head in the freakish Atlantic
Where it pours bean green over blue
In the waters off beautiful Nauset.
I used to pray to recover you.
Ach, du.

In the German tongue, in the Polish town
Scraped flat by the roller

Of wars, wars, wars.
But the name of the town is common.
My Polack friend

Says there are a dozen or two.
So I never could tell where you
Put your foot, your root,
I never could talk to you.
The tongue stuck in my jaw.

It stuck in a barb wire snare.
Ich, ich, ich, ich,
I could hardly speak.
I thought every German was you.
And the language obscene

An engine, an engine
Chuffing me off like a Jew.
A Jew to Dachau, Auschwitz, Belsen.
I began to talk like a Jew.
I think I may well be a Jew.

The snows of the Tyrol, the clear beer of Vienna
Are not very pure or true.
With my gypsy ancestress and my weird luck
And my Taroc pack and my Taroc pack
I may be a bit of a Jew.

I have always been scared of *you,*
With your Luftwaffe, your gobbledygoo.
And your neat moustache
And your Aryan eye, bright blue.
Panzer-man, panzer-man, O You——

Not God but a swastika
So black no sky could squeak through.
Every woman adores a Fascist,
The boot in the face, the brute
Brute heart of a brute like you.

You stand at the blackboard, daddy,
In the picture I have of you,
A cleft in your chin instead of your foot
But no less a devil for that, no not
Any less the black man who

Bit my pretty red heart in two.
I was ten when they buried you.
At twenty I tried to die
And get back, back, back to you.
I thought even the bones would do.

But they pulled me out of the sack,
And they stuck me together with glue.
And then I knew what to do.
I made a model of you,
A man in black with a Meinkampf look

And a love of the rack and the screw.
And I said I do, I do.
So daddy, I'm finally through.
The black telephone's off at the root,
The voices just can't worm through.

If I've killed one man, I've killed two——
The vampire who said he was you
And drank my blood for a year,
Seven years, if you want to know.
Daddy, you can lie back now.

There's a stake in your fat black heart
And the villagers never liked you.
They are dancing and stamping on you.
They always *knew* it was you.
Daddy, daddy, you bastard, I'm through.

LAST WORDS

I do not want a plain box, I want a sarcophagus
With tigery stripes, and a face on it
Round as the moon, to stare up.
I want to be looking at them when they come
Picking among the dumb minerals, the roots.
I see them already—the pale, star-distance faces.
Now they are nothing, they are not even babies.
I imagine them without fathers or mothers, like the first
     gods.
They will wonder if I was important.
I should sugar and preserve my days like fruit!
My mirror is clouding over—
A few more breaths, and it will reflect nothing at all.
The flowers and the faces whiten to a sheet.

I do not trust the spirit. It escapes like steam
In dreams, through mouth-hole or eye-hole. I can't stop it.
One day it won't come back. Things aren't like that.
They stay, their little particular lusters
Warmed by much handling. They almost purr.
When the soles of my feet grow cold,
The blue eye of my turquoise will comfort me.
Let me have my copper cooking pots, let my rouge pots
Bloom about me like night flowers, with a good smell.
They will roll me up in bandages, they will store my heart
Under my feet in a neat parcel.
I shall hardly know myself. It will be dark,
And the shine of these small things sweeter than the face
     of Ishtar.

James Hatch

LENORE KANDEL's books of poems include *The Love Book,* a highly controversial book openly celebrating sexual love, for which she went to trial in San Francisco, and *Word Alchemy,* from Grove Press. She writes of herself: "I was born under the sign of Capricorn, originally in New York City and later in Pennsylvania, Los Angeles, San Francisco and other occasions. I am no longer a professional belly dancer, school-bus driver, or choir singer. I stand witness for the divine animal and the possibility of the ecstatic access of enlightenment. My favorite word is YES!"

From: CIRCUS

Love in the
Middle of the Air

CATCH ME!
> I love you, I trust you,
> I love you
CATCH ME!
> catch my left foot, my right
> foot, my hand!
> here I am hanging by my teeth
> 300 feet up in the air and
CATCH ME!
> here I come, flying without wings,
> no parachute, doing a double triple
> super flip-flop somersault
> RIGHT UP HERE WITHOUT A
> SAFETY NET AND
CATCH ME!
> you caught me!
> I love you!

now it's *your* turn

Freak Show and Finale

xpose yourself!
ow me your tattooed spine and star-encrusted tongue!
dmit your feral snarl, your bloody jaws
ncede your nature and reveal your dreams!
> each beast contains its god, all gods are dreams
> all dreams are true

> LET THE BEAST WALK!!!!
permit the dog to fly, allow the spider love

e you the rainbow-headed child, the oracle of dream,
e witch of pain, the priest of tears, the door of love?

EXPOSE YOURSELF!
Are you the saint of lust, are you the beast that weeps?

EXPOSE YOURSELF!
Are you BOY 16 WEDS WOMAN 68 shaking with lu
Are you FATHER OF 3 SHOOTS SELF AND INFAN
    SON
Are you MANIAC BURNS LOVERS ALIVE
Are you UNKNOWN WOMAN LEAPS FROM BRIDG
Are you TEEN-AGE GIRL FOUND CHAINED IN
    ROOM
Are you half-man half-woman, do you weigh six hundre
    pounds, can you
walk on your hands, write with your toes, dance on a tigh
    wire?

EXPOSE YOURSELF!

    ACCEPT THE CREATURE
    AND BEGIN THE DANCE!

BLUES FOR SISTER SALLY

I

moon-faced baby with cocaine arms
        nineteen summers
        nineteen lovers

    novice of the junkie angel
    lay sister of mankind penitent
        sister in marijuana
        sister in hashish
        sister in morphine

against the bathroom grimy sink
pumping her arms full of life
        (holy holy)

he bears the stigma (holy holy) of the raving christ
(holy holy)
holy needle
holy powder
holy vein

dear miss lovelorn: my sister makes it with a hunk
of glass do you think this is normal miss lovelorn

I DEMAND AN ANSWER!

II

weep
for my sister she walks with open veins
leaving her blood in the sewers of your cities
from east coast
to west coast
to nowhere

how shall we canonize our sister who is not quite dead
who fornicates with strangers
who masturbates with needles
ho is afraid of the dark and wears her long hair soft and
black
against her bloodless face

III

midnight and the room dream-green and hazy
we are all part of the collage

brother and sister, she leans against the wall
and he, slipping the needle in her painless arm

pale fingers (with love) against the pale arm

IV

children our afternoon is soft, we lean against each oth

      our stash is in our elbows
      our fix is in our heads
god is a junkie and he has sold salvation
     for a week's supply

Shelley Lustig

JOANNE KYGER was born in Vallejo, California, November 19, 1934. She attended the University of California at Santa Barbara, although she left one unit short of her degree. She has lived in several countries, including China and India. Her published books are *The Tapestry and the Web* (1965), *To Anne* (1970), *Places to Go* (1970), and *Desecheo Notebook* (1971). She now lives in Bolinas, California.

*

In the high

clear air

it was icy

Did you Feel good?

I rose, I rose

above you a

Did you worry

how it could go
together? the one presses
against the other, and the trees cling
and the trees grow and the mountain

rises

the sk

changes around the sky

changes.

THE TIME IS OPEN

It's grey
today
and my thoughts
are of home
that can be mine
with other people
in this country
I transplant
my soul
to a place I say
I can love
Find the gods
eat the right food
love the body
the lungs
the feet
have children

America will not
be swept under me

For this time we have
not too much to lose
I don't have a husband
for a woman must cut
across the property bands
that hold this country
now this is the way
I think of it
to lay open my self
in ways that make
some sense for love

Cars pass
the sun begins
to show
I must start
these plans
The spirit
of calla lily
nasturtium
and rose

We are all
such plain people
and our voice is honest
and tries to search
for the tones
most natural to it here
on the coast

Every time he goes
I think I shall never
see him again
but it is not heart
break but such delight
and affirmation
when he returns

like sun
or spring
the numbers
of years

I'm exhilarated now, no
worry
Because I talked to the
owners of this house?
The septic tank
over flows
Mrs. Charles
Pepper's
Cabin of Dreams
brought over
by her mother
from the hill across
the street
Our waste again
which everybody lives with
and can't live
with the birds
that fly by
the window
wade in the lagoon
at the foot
of Pine Gulch Creek looking
for food that may not
be here
next year.   So they
these owners
put money in and build up
over the flat grasses that lead
down to the sea.

I'll leave this house
but not their worries
when I find my own.
Bumblebees, humming birds.

*

From this moment
and hence backwards
a visitation
echoes thru the apparent opening
to the tomb
the narrow passage is the mind's reasoning
in clarity
as she moves like a shadow
having lived her life before
it is now the particular graces
that surface
running amidst
that is not lighter than spring
water
is revealed
as the female
opens out
to receive
her own death, which is her own
eternal youth, her own love of herself.

Larry Basar

GRACE BUTCHER was born in Rochester, New York in 1934. She received her B.A. from Hiram College and her M.A. from Kent State University where she is now Instructor of English. She has been anthologized in *In a Time of Revolution* and *American Literary Anthology III,* and she received a grant from the National Endowment for the Arts in 1969. She has two booklets of poems, *More Stars Than Room For* and *The Bright-Colored Dark,* and a book of poems, *Rumors of Ecstasy, Rumors of Death,* was published by Ashland Poetry Press. A former U.S. track champion and record holder, she is still actively competing. She is married and has two sons.

WIFE OF THE MOON MAN
WHO NEVER CAME BACK

Often when the moon is full
they have to give her something
to make her sleep.
She confuses "moon" with "mine"
and has been known
to run naked on the lawn
screaming his name
and singing children's songs.
The familiar face
terrifies her.

Certain nights
she opens the curtains,
the windows,
opens her thighs,
her darkest places.
His body, thin silver now,
pours into her with no warmth;
her fingers crawl like animals
to their dark hole.

Thrilled and horrified,
she breathes the rush of silver air
with lungs that grow thick.
It is a familiar feeling:
the dust falling on her open eyes,
shadows or someone screaming,
caught in the surge of gigantic tides.

ON DRIVING BEHIND
A SCHOOL BUS FOR
MENTALLY RETARDED CHILDREN

Full deep green
bloom-fallen spring
here outside,
for us.

They,
like winter-covered crocuses:
strange bright beauty
peeping through snow
that never melts—

(How quietly,
how quietly,
the bus.)

These flowers have no fragrance.
They move to an eerie wind
I cannot feel.
They rise, with petals fully opened,
from a twisted seed,
and neither grow
nor wither.

They will be taught
the colors of their names.

ASSIGNMENT

Hey Mom!
(God said
let there be)
Gimme some
Flour & Water
(let the waters be)
I gotta Make
(let the dry land)
The World
It's due
Next week
(and there was evening)
Whatta mess
It's not even round
(and there was morning)
& it smells funny
Hey, could ya gimme
them Bride 'n Groom dolls
from your old cake
(male and female
he created)
They're kinda big
but I'll stick
their feet in good
(you are dust)
Wait'll the kids
(behold)
I bet Nobody Else
thought about
Making
(It was Very Good)
a World.

RESULTS OF THE POLO GAME

The young boys forget about cars awhile,
saunter carefully casual to touch the lathered shoulder,
wait for the sweet monotony of walking the wet ones dry.
The ponies are tough and tired and friendly,
walk docilely for a hundred different hands
around the circuit of cities and grass.
The young girls love easily:
the sweet smell of the silken coats,
the immense deep moving of hidden muscle,
the fumbling soft lips, the fine boney heads.

But the boys are slower, reluctant to react
to the uncoiling of this unfamiliar love.
They carry the smell in their nostrils for hours,
stronger, stranger than perfume or gasoline.
In bed before sleep they walk the wet horses,
the heads still loom at their shoulders,
their fingers curve to the sweated leather.
There is the neck to touch, to arch with the arm;
comparisons to make: a thousand pounds of power
held by thin reins, the alien metal in the soft mouth.

The thighs ache to curve around this new body.
There is confusion about the meanings of love,
embarrassment at boundaries that will not stay put,
ambiguous language that always leads to lust:
the curves, the shine, the power, the deep sweet smell,
the capturing, taming, gentling; the moving together.
The girls already know. Their thighs are open.
It is a satisfactory substitute, this love.
The boys, in sleep, run a hand through the thick mane,
lay their faces against a shining shoulder, and decide.

James Mitchell

DIANE DI PRIMA was born in 1934 in New York City and attended Swarthmore College. Her active involvement in contemporary poetry includes her work as editor of *The Floating Bear*, contributing editor of *Kulchur*, associate editor of *Signal Magazine*, and publisher and printer of The Poets Press. Her poetry includes *This Kind of Bird Flies Backward*, *Dinners and Nightmares*, *The New Handbook of Heaven*, *Poems for Freddie*, and *Revolutionary Letters*. She is the recipient of a grant from the National Institute of Arts and Letters.

233

From: REVOLUTIONARY LETTERS

dedicated to Bob Dylan

Revolutionary Letter #1

I have just realized that the stakes are myself
I have no other
ransom money, nothing to break or barter but my life
my spirit measured out, in bits, spread over
the roulette table, I recoup what I can
nothing else to shove under the nose of the *maître de jeu*
nothing to thrust out the window, no white flag
this flesh all I have to offer, to make the play with
this immediate head, what it comes up with, my move
as we slither over this go board, stepping always
(we hope) between the lines

Revolutionary Letter #4

Left to themselves people
grow their hair.
Left to themselves they
take off their shoes.
Left to themselves they make love
sleep easily
share blankets, dope & children
they are not lazy or afraid
they plant seeds, they smile, they
speak to one another. The word
coming into its own: touch of love
on the brain, the ear.

We return with the sea, the tides
we return as often as leaves, as numerous
as grass, gentle, insistent, we remember
the way,
our babes toddle barefoot thru the cities of the universe.

Revolutionary Letter #21

Can you
own land, can you
own house, own rights
to other's labor, (stocks, or factories
or money, loaned at interest)
what about
the yield of same, crops, autos
airplanes dropping bombs, can you
own real estate, so others
pay you rent? to whom
does the water belong, to whom
will the air belong, as it gets rarer?
the american indians say that a man
can own no more than he can carry away
on his horse.

THE QUARREL

You know I said to Mark that I'm furious at you.

No he said are you bugged. He was drawing Brad who was asleep on the bed.

Yes I said I'm pretty god damned bugged. I sat down by the fire and stuck my feet out to warm them up.

Jesus I thought you think it's so easy.   There you sit innocence personified. I didn't say anything else to him.

You know I thought I've got work to do too sometimes. In fact I probably have just as fucking much work to do as you do. A piece of wood fell out of the fire and I poked it back in with my toe.

I am sick I said to the woodpile of doing dishes. I am just
as lazy as you. Maybe lazier. The toe of my shoe was
scorched from the fire and I rubbed it where the suede was
gone.

Just because I happen to be a chick I thought.

Mark finished one drawing and looked at it. Then he put it
down and started another one.

It's damned arrogant of you I thought to assume that only
you have things to do. Especially tonight.

And what a god damned concession it was for me to bother
to tell you that I was bugged at all I said to the back of his
neck. I didn't say it out loud.

I got up and went into the kitchen to do the dishes. And
shit I thought I probably won't bother again. But I'll get
bugged and not bother to tell you and after a while everything will be awful and I'll never say anything because it's
so fucking uncool to talk about it. And that I thought will
be that and what a shame.

Hey hon Mark yelled at me from the living room. It says
here Picasso produces fourteen hours a day.

PRAYER TO THE MOTHERS

they say you lurk here still, perhaps
in the depths of the earth or on
some sacred mountain, they say
you walk (still) among men, writing signs
in the air, in the sand, warning warning weaving
the crooked shape of our deliverance, anxious
not hasty. Careful. You step among cups, step out o'
crystal, heal with the holy glow of your
dark eyes, they say you unveil

a green face in the jungle, wear blue
in the snows, attend on
births, dance on our dead, croon, fuck, embrace
our weariness, you lurk here still, mutter
in caves, warn, warn and weave
warp of our hope, link hands against
the evil in the stars, o rain
poison upon us, acid which eats clean
wake us like children from a nightmare, give the slip
to the devourers whom I cannot name
the metal men who walk
on all our substance, crushing flesh
to swamp

omo-di

SONIA SANCHEZ was born in Birmingham, Alabama in 1935. Her three books of poems are *Homecoming, We a BaddDDD People,* and *It's a New Day,* published by the Broadside Press. Her poems have appeared in *Negro Digest, Liberator, Journal of blk/poetry, Soulbook, Nommo, blk/ scholar,* and in *Broadside Series.* Her plays include *The Bronx Is Next* and *Dirty Hands.* She has lived in the San Francisco area, but she is currently living in New York City, teaching at Manhattan Community College and the University of Massachusetts at Amherst.

238

a poem for my father

how sad it must be
to love so many women
to need so many black
perfumed bodies weeping
underneath you.
                    when i remember all those nights
i filled my mind with
long wars between short
sighted trojans & greeks
while you slapped some
wide hips about in
your pvt dungeon,
when i remember your
deformity   i want to
do something about your
makeshift manhood.
i guess
          that is why
on meeting your sixth
wife, i cross myself
with her confessionals.

                —— answer to yo / question
            of am i not yo / woman
        even if u went on shit again ——

& i a beginner
                    in yo / love
say no.
          i wud not be yo / woman
& see u disappear
                    each day
befo my eyes
              and know yo /

reappearance
             to be
                   a one /
                          nite / stand.
no man.
         blk/
             lovers   cannot   live
in wite powder that removes
them from they blk/selves
                          cannot ride
majestic / wite / horses
                        in a machine age.
blk / lovers
            must live /
                        push against the
devils of this world
                     against the creeping
witeness of they own minds.
i am yo / woman
               my man.
                         and blk/women
deal in babies and
                   sweet / blk / kisses
and nites that
              multiply by twos.

personal letter no. 3

nothing will keep
us young you know
not young men or
women who spin
their youth on
cool playing sounds.
we are what we
are what we never
think we are.
no more wild geo

graphies of the
flesh. echoes. that
we move in tune
to slower smells.
it is a hard thing
to admit that
sometimes after midnight
i am tired
of it all.

Layle Silbert

SANDRA HOCHMAN was born in New York City, September 11, 1936. She received her B.A. from Bennington College and attended the Sorbonne in Paris and Columbia University. She has been an actress, but currently devotes herself full-time to writing. She received the Yale Younger Poets Award in 1965 for *Manhattan Pastures,* and her other books of poems are *Voyage Home, The Vaudeville Marriage, Love Letters from Asia,* and *Earthworks: Poems 1960–1970.*

242

FAREWELL POEMS

You never saw my rib cage. I would lie next to you
Breathing and my ribs would hardly be visible but
They would be there, shiny under the moon, the polished
Bones, and I would watch them go up and down but you
Would not see them. You were off somewhere else
　　dreaming
Of what would be, dreaming of alarms or the slow waking
Of the next day. I don't know what you were dreaming
But blatant as horns in the dream were my questions.

I was sleeping next to you. Fluids
Of my body were endless as ferns.
I contained the ocean and the river bed. I slept
Without waking. And when I woke I heard the snow
Outside the window.
What were we doing?

We were sleeping. Our legs touched.
But you never looked at my arms. You never saw my arms.
　　I had
Hidden them skillfully under a long robe during the
　　daytime
And I had used them to carry baskets and books and
　　flowers
In great brick pots. I had been housekeeping and
Then, before sleep, I rubbed the petals on my palms. And
Watched the endless snow fall down. Crystals in the dark
　　and
wanted to give you the gift of my very cold arms.

A HISTORY OF THE OPERA

It was summer on Boulevard Raspail.
Our bathroom walls were peeling to light pink,
Brushes and combs were missing teeth on

The bath shelves. A box of soapflakes
Stood by the bathtub waiting to transform me.

Tacked over the sink,
Painted de Kooning wenches torn
Out of *Art News* magazine
Were staring down. They didn't like
Being placed over the sink where no one
Knew who they were.

I looked like one of them: pouting, angry, hair always
    messed,
Spending afternoons inside the tub
Whenever my husband took off for more than a week
On a concert tour somewhere in Lisbon or Brussels
    Desperate—

I soaked in Paris. Scrubbing the loneliness
Of my skin. Frightened. I missed him
And needed the bubble baths to keep me from crying.
I sang in the daily bath. And thought sometimes of
    drowning.

Tub thoughts: when I was about fifteen
Some girls held a contest in boarding school to decide
The easiest way of suicide. A history major,
I quoted the Romans: "Bleeding in the bath—preferably
With slits in the arms. And loads of rose petals."
Tub thoughts: Paris—
It comes back
The bathtub filled with white detergent—Fab
Which made the bubbles in the tub as high
As an Eiffel Tower when I cried.

Now who was it
I really felt like drowning? Was it myself? My husband
Or de Kooning?—his
Painted American women screwed up and frustrated inside
    his mind,
Now paper witches hanging by my tub. American

'omen—locked in my bathroom—
'here they peered at my eyebrows, ears, and feet
'ithout the shrewdness that would make them great. O
hose young women—scrubbed and
ıbbed before they went to bed at night like children,
ashed, dressed, helped into pajamas,
ıcked into mighty dreams with creamy faces,
ıying their sexual prayers.
he painted women that I could not drown.

became aware of needing a lover
ne afternoon as I lay in the tub
nd stared at my knees. As I looked at my toes
ranted near rusty fixtures,
began thinking of a soap opera that might be called
Defense of Love.

hen chose my lover. A modest music teacher.
ımped out of the tub,
ıng him on the phone,
ıd finding him at home
here he happened to be writing *A History of the Opera,*
said, "All the pleasures
the opera are awaiting you."

entered the bathroom elegantly,
s dyed hair smoothed by pomade, the shiny strands
    greased black
er gray, his mustache
axed for this special occasion. To improvise: he joined
    me
the tub, where I awaited him
ıder the detergent
w easy! The ecstasy—
ır electrical field of water and shock,
e short-distance field
posing us to
ashcloth and soap.

Somehow I want to say—to get it "across to you"—ho
    moving
That bath was, the two of us sitting in my tub.
Those large soap bubbles in our mouths

And ice-water changes.
Our two bodies danced in a sea of detergent
And our dangerous arias.
There were no limitations to our city
When fables and swans
Splashed in the marble.

I cloaked him in a terry-cloth robe
And lifted him, gently, from the bath.
We turned and waved good-by
To the water.

De Kooning's maidens watched us back out of tl
    bathroom
As we slipped from their extraordinary reach.

THE SWIMMING POOL

Open me. Close me,
Shout the dangerous women
Sitting around the pool doing nothing.
Open me up, they are saying, their
Lips great pocketbooks
With shiny clasps. Inside the lobby
Ancient tourists sit
Dressed in nylon, talking
Lip to lip.

Under the secret flaps
Of beach cabanas
Ideograms pour over the
Women. Old numbers, letters
Fall on their hair and nails
As light lives in the pool.

THE GOLDFISH WIFE

It is Monday morning
And the goldfish wife
Comes out with her laundry
To shout her message.
There! Her basket glistens
In the sun and shines—
A wicker O. And see how
The goldfish wife touches
The clothes, her fingers
Stretching toward starch,
The wind beating her hair
As though all hair
Were laundry. Come,
Dear fishwife, golden
In your gills, come tell
Us of your life and be
Specific. Come into our lives—
Where no sun shines and no
Winds spill
The laundry from the rope—
Come on the broomstick of a
Widow-witch, fly
From the empty clotheslines
Of the poor
And teach us how to air
Our lives again.

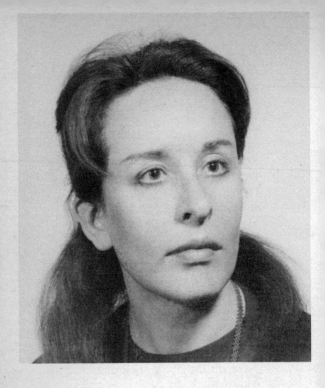

ROCHELLE OWENS was born in 1936. Her latest books of poetry include *Salt & Core*, Black Sparrow Press, and *I Am the Babe of Joseph Stalin's Daughter*, The Kulchur Foundation. Her highly innovative and controversial plays have been produced throughout this country, Canada and Europe, and a collection of five plays, *Futz and What Came After*, was published by Random House in 1968. She is one of the founding members of the New York Theatre Strategy, and is presently editing an anthology of new American plays, *Spontaneous Combustion!* She has given numerous poetry readings and recorded her adaptations of primitive and archaic world poetries.

WILD WOMAN'S
RESENTMENT OF FAKERY

You lousy bitch
you have insulted me
with my own grim
mythology
I guess this is
in the american scheme
of things   my betrayal.
My dear, I had visual-
ized you with perfect
woman's breasts breasts
of a damsel from the
northern renaissance
              your legs pressed
         together & wearing close-fitting
              animal skins, wild smell
         coming from your hands BIG as a drunken
      demon, a funny thought is playing
     about your fatal lips.
I notice something
ludicrous it makes
me dizzy what I notice
it doesn't fit in with
the picture I feel
nauseous
              I force you up against
         the 15th century tapestry like
      an American Indian. I'm hopping on a
     leg as I wind & hook a skein of your perfectly
   infuriating blonde hair around my fists
 pulling with my mighty strength!
              I believed you to be
         naturally blonde
         but you you
         dye your hair!

I am at the height of passionate conviction
as I kill you.
        I am a humorless bridegroom,
a mad-dog perfectionist.

ATATURK

She'd been biting her lips lately because of the sexua[l]
tension. It was Ataturk's fault though he was the greates[t]
she'd ever known. Was Sylvia a nympho? Not until sh[e]
met him.

Sylvia had never met a Turk before. Have you? Hav[e]
you? Well, Sylvia did (zowie, what a muscle-builder-com[-]
bination!) at "Chock full o' nuts." What a chest he ha[d]
got it from good food & drink, what a skull shape he ha[d]
molded like a Byelorussian's! And what a quantity [of]
energy! Very, very good. Thinking of the Philistine gian[t]
that Turk of Sylvia's made the inside of her thighs wet [a]
crude sugar; faint, weak too. He was drinking a cup [of]
coffee (the Turks brought it with them to Vienna, yo[u]
know) & eating a brownie. When she sat next to him sh[e]
started whiffing the harbor of Istanbul, perfume, hea[t]
stroke, headless chickens. Sylvia smelled that man out li[ke]
a mouse ripe cheese; what a fat pleasure for a girl in lov[e]
. . . Sylvia fell in love right on that "Chock full o' nut[s]
stool & Ataturk did likewise! Sing, speak, that's what [he]
did with his golden-brown eyes, for ten minutes! While [he]
looked at her, while he just looked at her! She sang bac[k]
at him (while the counter-people stared) her high-pries[t-]
esses' membranic song. Ataturk stuffed her in his eyeba[ll]
& balanced her on his brain. A thin high squeal came o[ut]
of his throat making her feel crazy.

'Ataturk's such a masculine name', thought Sylvia. Sh[e]
bit her lips again, the goddamned tension. The end of h[er]
cigarette had a mixture of blood & lipstick . . . I can't t[ell]
you the sex side of their story but well, it was like the i[n-]
side of a bluish lilac. 'Atagirl', thought Sylvia. 'Very goo[d]

THE SKY-SPLITTING
PINK RUBBER BISTRO

One wants to be sitting in
    maybe in Vienna I want
      to be in Vienna in
        a bistro
          made of sky-splitting
            pink rubber
when she walks in
      I appear (formerly Henry
            Miller)
        now I'm a flickering
          spyder-eyed
bottle-shaped breasted
           portable electric-
        lighted gunpowdered
        hearted
            beauty!
I'm a burst-of-light-woman
        Wow!
           Her teeth
clamp into my neck I see her round
    persian melon dusky
hips f l o a t i n g past
              my eyes
    like hot red letters spelling
scudda hoo scudda hay
       what a beautiful woman
to buckle my knees for
          to forever
    trail after
         I am Henry
     Miller turned,
ReInCaRnAtEd into a
        beautiful girl!

I read Sanscrit on
           her tit & function
   as the U.S. government
all encompassing like the chinese wall
    I hold the girl
      & fence her in
  to my golden fruit heart
    we speak Viennese
together & eat little
            cakes
she says I should be
        Poet Laureate
of Vienna China!
& I should teach the love of magic
     & girls
   in a bistro
made of sky-splitting
       pink rubber!

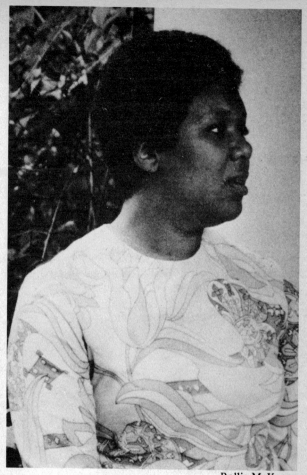

Rollie McKenna

LUCILLE CLIFTON was born in 1936 in Depew, New York. She attended Howard University and Fredonia State Teachers College. Her books of poems are *Good Times* (1969) and *Good News About the Earth* (1972). The mother of six children, she is also the author of three children's books.

MISS ROSIE

When I watch you
wrapped up like garbage
sitting, surrounded by the smell
of too old potato peels
or
when I watch you
in your old man's shoes
with the little toe cut out
sitting, waiting for your mind
like next week's grocery
I say
when I watch you
you wet brown bag of a woman
who used to be the best looking gal in Georgia
used to be called the Georgia Rose
I stand up
through your destruction
I stand up

*

If I stand in my window
naked in my own house
and press my breasts
against my windowpane
like black birds pushing against glass
because I am somebody
in a New Thing

and if the man come to stop me
in my own house
naked in my own window
saying I have offended him
I have offended his

Gods

let him watch my black body
push against my own glass
let him discover self
let him run naked through the streets
crying
praying in tongues

THE LOST BABY POEM

the time i dropped your almost body down
down to meet the waters under the city
and run one with the sewage to the sea
what did i know about waters rushing back
what did i know about drowning
or being drowned

you would have been born into winter
in the year of the disconnected gas
and no car   we would have made the thin
walk over Genesee hill into the Canada wind
to watch you slip like ice into strangers' hands
you would have fallen naked as snow into winter
if you were here i could tell you these
and some other things

if i am ever less than a mountain
for your definite brothers and sisters
let the rivers pour over my head
let the sea take me for a spiller
of seas   let black men call me stranger
always   for your never named sake

NANCY WILLARD was born June 26, 1936. She
is married to Eric Lindbloom and they have one son.
She is now teaching in the English Department at
Vassar College. Her book of essays on Rilke, Neruda,
Williams and Ponge is *Testimony of the Invisible
Man*, University of Missouri Press. Her books of
poems include *The Lively Anatomy of God*, Eakins
Press; *Skin of Grace*, University of Missouri Press;
In His Country, Generation New Poets, Ann Arbor,
Michigan; and *19 Masks for the Naked Poet*, Kayak.

THE POET'S WIFE MAKES HIM A DOOR
SO HE CAN FIND THE WAY HOME.

Nobody else makes doors like the poet's wife.

If she made a revolving door,
summer and winter would run like mice in a wheel.
If she made a door for the moon,
the dead would cross over alive.

Each door is a mirror.

So when the poet loses his way,
crossing the desert in search of his heart,
his wife hoists her lintels and straw on her back
and sets out, feeling his grief with her feet.

She calls up a door that shimmers like water.

She unfolds her palm trees and parrots.
And far away, his belly dredging the dunes,
the poet hears his heart spinning
straw into gold for the sun.

The palms bow. The parrots are calling his name.

He remembers the way home.

CLEARING THE AIR

It's been ten years since you tried to kill me.
Biking home one night, I saw only your legs
stepping behind a tree, then you fell on my throat
like a cat.   My books crashed the birds out of sleep.
We rolled in the leaves like lovers.   My eyes popped
like Christmas lights, veins snapped, your teeth wore

my blood, your fingers left bars on my neck.
I can't remember your name,
and I saw your face only in court.
You sat in a box, docile as old shoes.
And I, who had never felt any man's weight
sometimes felt yours for nights afterwards.

Well, I'm ready to forgive
and I don't want to forget.
Sometimes I tell myself that we met
differently, on a train.   You give me
a batman comic and show me your passport.
I have nothing but my report card,

but I offer my mother's fudge for the grapes
rotting the one paper bag you carry.
In my tale you are younger and loved.
Outside you live in a thousand faces
and so do your judges, napping in parks,
rushing to fires, folded like bats on the truck,

mad and nude in a white Rolls
pinching dollars and leather behinds.
Burned from a tree by your betters, you take
to the streets and hang in the dark like a star,
making me see your side, waking me
with the blows and the weight of it.

MARRIAGE AMULET

You are polishing me like old wood.
At night we curl together like two rings
on a dark hand.   After many nights,
the rough edges wear down.

If this is aging, it is warm as fleece.
I will gleam like ancient wood.

I will wax smooth, my crags and cowlicks
well-rubbed to show my grain.

Some sage will keep us in his hand for peace.

THE FREAK SHOW

I am Giuletta, the bird woman.   I married
the rain man and learned to fly.
Together we walked the high wire
over trees, churches, bridges, green fields,
straight into heaven.   We saw the white seed
after a child blows it, and were much praised.
Though I had nothing but him, I craved no more.

Even in falling he blazed like a star.
The next night I went on, knowing I could not fall.
A brave girl, the clowns told me.   Then I cried.
I knew that people who never fall forget
danger is all and their blood goes dumb.
Listen, the ring-man said to me one night,
You've lost your shape.   You've got no grace.
You're old.

Waiting in the dark trucks I am content to watch,
to nibble the sweet fruits that the dwarf brings,
We walk among the orchards and hear
the silence of tensed feet on the blessed wire.
So much walking affects the appetite, Madam,
says the dwarf with a sucking leer.
And so much sorrow gives enormous hunger.

I am round and simple as a Persian plum,
so earth-shaped now no wire could hold me
or support the weight of my fallow grief.
When you hear the dwarf crying the measure

of my marvelous flesh, you will crowd in.
Blinded by footlights, I hear you wallow
and whisper in the pit below my chair.

My God!   Arms like tree trunks cries a man's voice
Must be hard on the heart, a woman blurts.
O friends, it is very hard on the heart
For your delight I devour loaf after loaf
of stale bread, till the silken tents sink to rest
and wide-eyed children, bogeyed to bed,
remember my cavernous mouth with fear.

Sometimes I pick at my food like a child.
The taste of the wire in the apple hurts.

FOR YOU, WHO DIDN'T KNOW

At four a.m. I dreamed myself on that beach
where we'll take you after you're born.
I woke in a wave of blood.

Lying in the backseat of a nervous Chevy
I counted the traffic lights, lonely as planets.
Starlings stirred in the robes of Justice

over the Town Hall.   Miscarriage of justice,
they sang, while you, my small client
went curling away like smoke under my ribs.

Kick me!   I pleaded.   Give me a sign
that you're still there!
Train tracks shook our flesh from our bones.

Behind the hospital rose a tree of heaven.
    You can learn something from everything
        a rabbi told his hasidim who did not believe it.

I didn't believe it, either, O rabbi,
what did you learn on the train to Belsen?
That because of one second one can miss everything.

There are rooms on this earth for emergencies.
A sleepy attendant steals my clothes and my name,
and leaves me among the sinks on an altar of fear.
Your name. Your name. Sign these papers,
authorizing us in our wisdom to save the child.
Sign here for circumcision. Your faith, your faith."

O rabbi, what can we learn from the telegraph?
asked the hasidim, who did not understand.
And he answered, *That every word is counted and
charged.*

This is called a dobtone," smiles the doctor.
He greases my belly, stretched like a drum
and plants a microphone there, like a flag.

A thousand thumping rabbits! Savages clapping for joy!
My heart dancing its name, I'm-here, I'm-here!
The cries of fishes, of stars, the tunings of hair!

O rabbi, what can we learn from a telephone?
*My schicksa daughter, your faith, your faith
that what we say here is heard there.*

DEENA METZGER was born in 1936. She was Drama and Arts Editor for the *Los Angeles Free Press* on two separate occasions, and is currently a member of the Critical Studies Department at the California Institute of the Arts. She has just completed her third novel, and her poems, articles, reviews, and selections from her novels have appeared in various journals. She is the founding member and chairman of Our Free School. She has two sons.

A TALISMAN FOR THE NEW YEAR

We grind horns
till there are no more unicorns
to grind,
Then stand embarrassed
without our magic
as Eve
finding herself again in Eden
is equally unprepared.

There is no healing our condition
with beauty dead

Think of the beast:
He sweated
and his hide turned gray
and mudstained as
he copulated in the field
like the rest of us.
He was foolish for women
particularly young ones
seeking to trap his beauty
in an exchange of thorns.

Christmas is never a problem.
It's the resurrection that's difficult,
that's hard to do right,
making death into flesh again
trading stone for a living horn.

The Unicorn is dead
crowned with carrots.
His horn wilts like
a white root.
Beauty is a wound
without dimension.
Magic is a celluloid eye.

The beast is dead
where the millstone
is a platter
for dry condiments
of lace and bugles
and cherry tapestries
and damask laps.

The well is poisoned
We neither drink
nor eat
nor mourn.
It's a hard measure
to abandon form.

The Unicorn is dead.
And it's the resurrection,
the raising of the beast
That is the bitch.
No virgin tresses
nor princely gait
gets him second time around.

It's   a bellow
that raises up this beast
who is not gentle,
It's a clay hand, hot,
that encounters the horn.

Raise up the beast
Who is not gentle
        Bellowing
Who sweats in the field
        Bellowing
Who is the issue of thistle
        Bellowing
Who has magic
        Bellowing
(we all do)
Locked in his horn.

LITTLE LEAGUE WOMEN

The women are larger than I
fed on beefsteak and beer
guzzled from nippled bottles
like Jap cows
in a film I saw once.
Their flanks ripple with fat
above thin hoofs.

The women take it from the earth first.
The juices flow up and make milk
to dribble in one and another
goat red mouth.
Yet the kids are thin
as stalks and corn blond.

The women grow
beyond comfort,
nimble only when surprised.
There is nothing sympathetic about them
They sweat under their breasts
and swat flies.

Herding in dumb bulk,
the women are cows
eating grass and men.
What cud there is
once chewed
is spit.

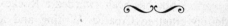

JUNE JORDAN was born in Harlem in 1936 and
grew up in the Bedford-Stuyvesant section of Brooklyn. She says, "I have learned how to fight and I am
learning how to love. I am working hard and I hope
my work will help us win liberation from the hatred
and death-worshipping, joyless powers that rule too
much of the world." She has been awarded a Rocke-
feller Foundation grant in Creative Writing and a
Prix de Rome in Environment Design. Her books,
published since 1969, include: *Who Look At Me,
Soulscript, The Voice of the Children, Some Changes,
His Own Where, Dry Victories,* and *Mrs. Fannie
Lou Hamer.* She is currently teaching film-making
in addition to her work as a poet and writer of fiction.

OKAY "NEGROES"

Okay "Negroes"
American Negroes
looking for milk
crying out loud
in the nursery of freedomland:
the rides are rough.
Tell me where you got that image
of a male white mammy.
God is vague and he don't take no sides.
You think clean fingernails crossed legs a smile
shined shoes
a crucifix around your neck
good manners
no more noise
you think who's gonna give you something?

Come a little closer.
Where you from?

POEM FOR MY FAMILY:
HAZEL GRIFFIN AND
VICTOR HERNANDEZ CRUZ

Dedicated to Robert Penn Warren

I

December 15, 1811
a black, well-butchered slave
named George took leave of Old Kentucky—true
he left that living hell in pieces—
first his feet fell to the fire
and the jelly of his eyes lay smoking
on the pyre a long while—

but he burned complete
at last he left at least he got away.
The others had to stay there
where he died like meat
(that slave)

how did he live?

December 15, 1811

Lilburn Lewis and his brother
cut and killed somebody real
because they missed their mother:
Thomas Jefferson's sweet sister Lucy
Correction: Killed no body: killed a slave
the time was close to Christmas sent the poor
black bastard to the snow zones of a blue-eyed
heaven and he went the way he came like meat
not good enough to eat
not nice enough to see
not light enough to live
he came the way he went like meat.

POEM FOR 175 Pounds
("Poor George")

II

Southern Kentucky, Memphis, New Orleans,
Little Rock, Milwaukee, Brooklyn, San Antonio,
Chicago, Augusta.
I am screaming
do you hear the pulse
destroying properties
of your defense against me and my life
now what are you counting
dollar bills or lives?
How did you put me down
as property?
as life?
How did you describe the damage?
I am naked
I am Harlem and Detroit

currently knives and bullets
I am lives
YOUR PROPERTY IS DYING
I am lives
MY LIFE IS BEING BORN
This is a lesson
in American History
What can you teach me?
The fire smells of slavery.

III

Here is my voice the speed and the wondering
darkness of my desire is
all that I am here
all that you never allowed:
I came and went like meat not good enough to eat
remember no remember
yes remember me
the shadow following your dreams
the human sound that never reached your ears
that disappear
vestigial
when the question is my scream
and I am screaming
whiteman
do you hear the loud
the blood, the real hysteria of birth
my life is being born
your property is dying

IV

What can you seize
from the furnace
what can you save?
America
I mean America how
do you intend to incinerate
my slavery?

I have taken my eyes from the light of your fires.
The begging body grows cold.
I see.
I see my self
Alive
A life

AND WHO ARE YOU?

I

Leave my eyes
alone
why should I make
believe this place entirely

is white
and I am nothing

pasted to a fantasy
(big black phallus
wide white teeth)
of particles you
blast to pieces asking me
to swallow them as
monster bits

That bit is me.

and even if I wave my arms no
rules will stop the traffic
stop the hatred running near
with ropes and mongrels
on the mind blind cloth
and bloodhounds
at the cradle

II

Don't tell me windmills
like the color of maroon
which was OK
when I first saw a zebra

that's the color of her coat
and in the hallway where she
waits for money once a week
she pulls a spool
of silk along the needles

for a doily

don't tell me windmills
turn no more just
like the horse
that used to lead
the trolleys   you can't
help but smell four legs the
board above for two and hear him
bargaining to tune bananamato
peachpotato   awk   awk
parsley

nothing goes too fast

old fish and unwashed hair why
don't he cut the screwing get
him something nice   sits
on the step a
nylon stocking cap to
cover up his head the cat
fastidious outside
the room
of his secondhand bed

III

Old fish and unwashed hair
you may surmise by reading
the windows
bandaged with the Daily
News from World War
Two which anyway was not the first
that

nothing goes too fast

but slowly like the windmill
like the good milord
and Uncle Remus for a hero

O merrily the children
suffered verily the elevator
Boys with buttons
from the Army and the cleaning
Girls of fifty-five
                    "the children"
suffered as they came to
hear the wild and holy
black book out of the mouths
of the mob and underneath
a hanging tree

IV

Take the acolyte
obsequious and horsey
under lace
            on Monday
off the altar

on the stoop

and no more candles

in the vestibule a no
watt testicle just dangles

take the acolyte his
yellhello for girls his
little sister slow with shoes from '66
a blue harmonica inside her mouth o
sweetly play that Jesu Joy of
Man's Desiring and Desiring and desiring
she
should comb her hair at least or he
could screw forgiveness
for a change move
over but
don't tell me
drums and muscle

on the stoop

sit-in on the stoop
museum
tombstone of the horse maroon
dark dais insane sanctum
if you make it you play ball
       talk loud
       speak low
       drink cheap
       tell lies
       LOOK AT THE PEOPLE

HE LOOKS LIKE A MAN
HE LOOKS LIKE ONE

MARGE PIERCY was born in 1936, and now lives in Wellfleet, Massachusetts. She has written two novels, *Going Down Fast* and *Dance the Eagle to Sleep,* and her books of poetry include *Breaking Camp* and *Hard Loving,* both published by the Wesleyan University Press. She is also included in a book with three other poets, *4-Telling,* Crossing Press. She is currently working on a new novel which involves about ten years in the lives of two women. She says about herself: "The first twenty-five years of my life had little to offer besides poverty, and hassles, and scrabbling to survive. I worked for years in various organizations of the New Left, before I came into women's liberation three years ago. The women's movement is healing together the various fragments of my life, my work, my politics, my pain, giving me feedback and constituency and often a kick in the teeth."

From: WALKING INTO LOVE

Meditation in my favorite position

Peace, we have arrived.
The touch point
where words end
and body goes on.
That's all:
finite, all five-sensual
and never repeatable.
Know you and be known,
please you and be pleased
in act:
the antidote to shame
is nakedness together.
Words end,
body goes on
and something
small and wet and real
is exchanged

THE FRIEND

We sat across the table.
he said, cut off your hands.
they are always poking at things.
they might touch me.
I said yes.

Food grew cold on the table.
he said, burn your body.
it is not clean and smells like sex.
it rubs my mind sore.
I said yes.

I love you, I said.
that's very nice, he said
I like to be loved,
that makes me happy.
Have you cut off your hands yet?

COUNCILS

We must sit down
and reason together.
We must sit down:
men standing want to hold forth.
They rain down upon faces lifted.
We must sit down on the floor
on the earth
on stones and mats and blankets.
There must be no front to the speaking
no platform, no rostrum,
no stage or table.
We will not crane
to see who is speaking.
Perhaps we should sit in the dark.
In the dark we could utter our feelings.
In the dark we could propose
and describe and suggest.
In the dark we could not see who speaks
and only the words
would say what they say.
No one would speak more than twice.
No one would speak less than once.
Thus saying what we feel and what we want,
what we fear for ourselves and each other
into the dark, perhaps we could begin
to begin to listen.
Perhaps we should talk in groups
the size of new families,
not more, never more than twenty.
Perhaps we should start by speaking softly.

women must learn to dare to speak.
men must learn to bother to listen.
women must learn to say I think this is so.
men must learn to stop dancing solos on the ceiling.
each speaks, she or he
say a ritual phrase:
not I who speaks but the wind.
d blows through me.
g after me, is the wind.

EMBRYOS

1. *Wee*

I am thin as nail parings. Light as dandruff.
When I cry I listen to myself,
pages of Bible paper turning over.

Who will love my morning toadstool sighs?
My rubber lusts sway like sea anemones.
My hatreds mew once and stifle, still blind.

will zip my mouth and put mittens on my hands
nd innocent and eggstill I will wait.
On a teatray my vanilla prince will come.

2. *Whey*

Why do you cry? No one comes.
am waiting in the grey to be born.

our legs are driftwood.
our face is a pike's.
our touch rusts.
Why do you rub the mirror?
How could my hair thin when no one pulled it?
Whose fingers pressed in my cheeks?
What mousemouth sucked my breasts?

My shadow limps from the window baaing.
Fog is in me.

Who are you crying for? Ash
in the chimney flue.
The sun to fatten my shrunk shadow.
Quick, bear me: my gourd chest shakes.
The clock trickles sand on my forehead.
I am dry as onions.

See the sun's fatherly eye
opening to heat me.
Today is my right birthday.

Bury her.

RIGHT THINKING MAN

The head: egg of all.
He thinks of himself as a head thinking.
He is eating a coddled egg.
He drops a few choice phrases on his wife,
who cannot seem to learn after twenty years
the perfection of egg protein
neither runny nor turned to rubber.
He drinks orange juice sweated from migrant labor.
Their children have pot bellies of hunger.
He drinks coffee from the colony of Brazil.
Advancing into his study he dabbles a forefinger
in the fine dust on his desk and calls his wife
who must go twitching to reprimand
the black woman age 48 who cleans the apartment.
Outside a Puerto Rican in a uniform
is standing in the street to guard his door
from the riffraff who make riots on television
in which the university who pays him owns much s
Right thinking is virtue, he believes,
and the clarity of the fine violin of his mind
leads him a tense intricate fugue of pleasure.

s children do not think clearly.
ey snivel and whine and glower and pant
er false gods who must be blasted with sarcasm
ain and again because their barbaric heads
ep growing back in posters on bedroom walls.
s wife does not dare to think.
married her for her breasts
d soft white belly of surrender
hing up like a puppy.
inking defines the human:
duty is to think.
ny is the brat nextdoor making those noises?
e greatest pain he has ever known
s in the dentist's office
ting an impacted wisdom tooth out.
e greatest suffering he ever tasted
s when he failed to get the fellowship
had counted on and had planned his itinerary.
en he curses his dependents
to sits on his right hand and Aristotle on his left.
gument is lean red meat to him.
ses and Freud and Dr. Johnson are in his corner.
is a good man and deserves to judge us all
o go making uncouth noises and bangs in the street.
is a good man: if you don't believe me,
any god.
says they all think like him.

JUDY GRAHN is now living in Oakland, California.
She has written one book, *Edward the Dyke and
Other Poems*. She says of her picture: "One time
Wendy and I were stranded in a bus station at 4:30
in the morning, so to entertain ourselves we took
some pictures. As this one clearly shows, we are
insane, evil and devious. All the other women we
know are like that too." In the above picture, Judy
is on the right.

THE COMMON WOMAN

I. *Helen, at 9 am, at noon, at 5:15*

r ambition is to be more shiny
d metallic, black and purple as
hief at midday; trying to make it
a male form, she's become as
f as possible.
aring trim suits and spike heels,
 says "bust" instead of breast;
newhere underneath she
sses love and trust, but she feels
t spite and malice are the
ces of success. She doesnt realize
, that she's missed success, also,
her smile is sometimes still
uine. After a while she'll be a real
er, bitter and more wily, better at
ing the men against each other
getting the other women fired.
 constantly conspires.
r grief expresses itself in fits of fury
r details, details take the place of meaning,
ney takes the place of life.
 believes that people are lice
 eat her, so she bites first; her
st increases year by year and by the time
sheen has disappeared from her black hair,
 tension makes her features unmistakably
, she'll go mad. No one in particular
 care. As anyone who's had her for a boss
 know
common woman is as common
he common crow.

II. *Ella, in a square apron, along Highway 80*

She's a copperheaded waitress,
tired and sharp-worded, she hides
her bad brown tooth behind a wicked
smile, and flicks her ass
out of habit, to fend off the pass
that passes for affection.
She keeps her mind the way men
keep a knife—keen to strip the game
down to her size. She has a thin spine,
swallows her eggs cold, and tells lies.
She slaps a wet rag at the truck drivers
if they should complain. She understands
the necessity for pain, turns away
the smaller tips, out of pride, and
keeps a flask under the counter. Once,
she shot a lover who misused her child.
Before she got out of jail, the courts had pounced
and given the child away. Like some isolated lake,
her flat blue eyes take care of their own stark
bottoms. Her hands are nervous, curled, ready
to scrape.
The common woman is as common
as a rattlesnake.

III. *Nadine, resting on her neighbor's stoop*

She holds things together, collects bail,
makes the landlord patch the largest holes.
At the Sunday social she would spike
every drink, and offer you half of what she knows,
which is plenty. She pokes at the ruins of the city
like an armored tank; but she thinks
of herself as a ripsaw cutting through

ots in wood. Her sentences come out
e thick pine shanks
d her big hands fill the air like smoke.
e's a mud-chinked cabin in the slums,
ting on the doorstep counting
s and raising 15 children,
lf of them her own. The neighborhood
uld burn itself out without her;
e of these days she'll strike the spark herself.
e's made of grease
d metal, with a hard head
at makes the men around her seem frail.
e common woman is as common as
ail.

IV. *Carol, in the park,*
chewing on straws

She has taken a woman lover
whatever shall we do
she has taken a woman lover
how lucky it wasnt you

d all the day through she smiles and lies
l grits her teeth and pretends to be shy,
weak, or busy. Then she goes home
l pounds her own nails, makes her own
s, and fixes her own car, with her friend.
e goes as far
women can go without protection
m men.

weekends, she dreams of becoming a tree;
ree that dreams it is ground up
l sent to the paper factory, where it
helpless in sheets, until it dreams
becoming a paper airplane, and rises
its own current; where it turns into a
l, a great coasting bird, that dreams of becoming

more free, even, than that—a feather, finally, or
a piece of air with lightning in it.
> she has taken a woman lover
> whatever can we say
She walks around all day
quietly, but underneath it
she's electric;
angry energy inside a passive form.
The common woman is as common
as a thunderstorm.

V. *Detroit Annie, hitchhiking*

Her words pour out as if her throat were a broken
artery and her mind were cut glass, carelessly handl
You imagine her in a huge velvet hat with great
dangling black feathers,
but she shaves her head instead
and goes for three-day midnight walks.
Sometimes she goes down to the dock and dances
off the end of it, simply to prove her belief
that people who cannot walk on water
are phonies, or dead.
When she is cruel, she is very, very
cool and when she is kind she is lavish.
Fishermen think perhaps she's a fish, but they're all
fools. She figured out that the only way
to keep from being frozen was to
stay in motion, and long ago converted
most of her flesh into liquid. Now when she
smells danger, she spills herself all over,
like gasoline, and lights it.
She leaves the taste of salt and iron
under your tongue, but you don't mind.
The common woman is as common
as the reddest wine.

VI. *Margaret, seen through a picture window*

After she finished her first abortion
she stood for hours and watched it spinning in the
toilet, like a pale stool.
Some distortion of the rubber
doctors with their simple tubes and
complicated prices,
still makes her feel guilty.
White and yeasty.
All her broken bubbles push her down
into a shifting tide, where her own face
floats above her like the whole globe.
She lets her life go off and on
in a slow strobe.
At her last job she was fired for making
strikes, and talking out of turn;
now she stays home, a little blue around the edges.
Counting calories and staring at the empty
magazine pages, she hates her shape
and calls herself overweight.
Her husband calls her a big baboon.
Lusting for changes, she laughs through her
teeth, and wanders from room to room.
The common woman is as solemn as a monkey
or a new moon.

VII. *Vera, from my childhood*

Solemnly swearing, to swear as an oath to you
who have somehow gotten to be a pale old woman;
swearing, as if an oath could be wrapped around your
    shoulders
like a new coat:
For your 28 dollars a week and the bastard boss
you never let yourself hate;
and the work, all the work you did at home

where you never got paid;
For your mouth that got thinner and thinner
until it disappeared as if you had choked on it,
watching the hard liquor break your fine husband down
into a dead joke.
For the strange mole, like a third eye
right in the middle of your forehead;
for your religion which insisted that people
are beautiful golden birds and must be preserved;
for your persistent nerve
and plain white talk—
the common woman is as common
as good bread
as common as when you couldn't go on
but did.
For all the world we didn't know we held in common
all along
the common woman is as common as the best of bread
and will rise
and will become strong—I swear it to you
I swear it to you on my own head
I swear it to you on my common
woman's
head

*

I have come to claim
Marilyn Monroe's body
for the sake of my own.
dig it up, hand it over,
cram it in this paper sack.
hubba. hubba. hubba.
look at those luscious
long brown bones, that wide and crusty
pelvis. ha HA, oh she wanted so much to be serious
but she never stops smiling now.
Has she lost her mind?

Marilyn, be serious—they're taking
your picture, and they're taking the pictures
of eight young women in New York City
who murdered themselves for being pretty
by the same method as you, the very
next day, after you!
I have claimed their bodies too,
they smile up out of my paper sack
like brainless cinderellas.

The reporters are furious, they're asking
me questions
what right does a woman have
to Marilyn Monroe's body?   and what
am I doing for lunch? They think I
mean to eat you.   Their teeth are lurid
and they want to pose me, leaning
on the shovel, nude.   Don't squint.
But when one of the reporters comes too close
I beat him, bust his camera
with your long, smooth thigh
and with your lovely knucklebone
I break his eye.

Long ago you wanted to write poems.
Be serious, Marilyn
I am going to take you in this paper sack
around the world, and
write on it:—the poems of Marilyn Monroe—
Dedicated to all princes,
the male poets who were so sorry to see you go,
before they had a crack at you.
They wept for you, and also
they wanted to stuff you
while you had a little meat left
in useful places;
but they were too slow.

Now I shall take them my paper sack
and we shall act out a poem together:
"How would you like to see Marilyn Monroe,
in action, smiling, and without her clothes?"
We shall wait long enough to see them make familiar faces
and then I shall beat them with your skull.
hubba. hubba. hubba. hubba. hubba.
Marilyn, be serious
Today I have come to claim your body for my own.

Max Yeh

LYNN SUKENICK was born on D. H. Lawrence's
birthday, September 11, but in 1937. She says,
"Raised in New York and stayed put till I was eighteen. Then a great deal of movement—Boston, San
Francisco, New York, Europe, the woods of Connecticut, Ithaca, now Southern California where I teach
writing and literature at the University of California at
Irvine. Poetics? I want to bring to the law and order
of existence the chaos of poetry." She is a collagist
as well as a poet, and her work appeared in a group
show at the Archifleur Gallery in Paris, 1970–71.

THE POSTER

I

He does not have the experiences
which are in his poems.
He'll compete
under any conditions.
He is wanted by more women than any other man,
for the mustache
hidden in his mustache.
He gets away with it.
He goes by the name of "Winner".
Watch out for him.

2

He speaks to me with his knuckles
on my head.
He tells me I am boring.
He hollows out a space inside my chest
as a whittler would do it,
carefully, coolly,
whistling a tune
everyone knows and likes.
He ties up my body
to be shipped somewhere
in a heavy string
and greasy brown butcherpaper.
He is blond
as a nazi.
Each time he looks at me with his frosty eyes
an animal dies in the local forest
and someone puts on a uniform.

THAT LIFE, ON FILM

My mother,
a snail in black velvet,
keeps her back to the
camera.
My father, the wolf
who sipped up the lake,
saved a drop for his daughter
and a bubble the size of a toad
for his son,
looks on.
He speaks of the cat:
how he doesn't want it,
how he hasn't taken it to the vet
for a reason chopped from the plot.

My mother stirs on the couch
like a breast in sleep.
He sees, and shows her
his face of ice.
You cannot see
what he does with his hands
(for it isn't
nice) but he
holds me,
like a dish of fat
for the gods;
murmurs
I am worthy,
I am
pure gold
(for the gods)
and that is why he will leave me here.
He bends
and puts me into the fire.
His head blots out the shrivelling clouds,
blots up
the whole picture.

DEATH

A small
bottle
of blackish
fluid
with a match
floating in it:
understand
its qualities
as well as its appearance:
make your mind
a hospital.
Feel ill a little;
an accident with your hip
will help;
the terminal's not an
exploding car
but a soiled bed
with your body on it,
a boy forgetting
to empty the fishtank.

A girl will phone
with a free subscription
the instant after
the motion begins,
but the doors of the ballroom
are black as the shoes
that have taken you there.
You are not exempt:
whatever his clothes are
you dance;
you *move;*
he is faster than you are.

EARLY ELLA

for Ella Fitzgerald

Her voice
slips through our ears
like your arm through mine.

She is the net,
the fish,
and the water.

She sings like women
            swimming,
a bell inside her
            dipping,
            gonging,
like a buoy.

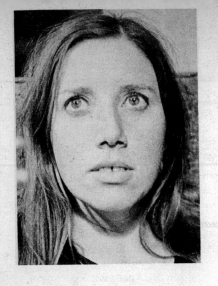

KATHLEEN FRASER was born in 1937 in Tulsa, Oklahoma, and received her B.A. from Occidental College. She began writing in her senior year in college and then worked at *Mademoiselle* as an assistant editor. She joined a poetry workshop taught by Stanley Kunitz and later studied under Kenneth Koch at the New School for Social Research. Her work was included in the first *Young American Poets* anthology edited by Paul Carroll, and she won the Dylan Thomas Poetry Award from the New School in 1967. She has taught at San Francisco State College, the University of Iowa, and Reed College. Her books of poems are *Change of Address, In Defiance (of the Rains), Little Notes to You from Lucas Street,* and a book of children's poems and game chants based on Brueghel's painting "Children Playing Games" called *Stilts, Somersaults & Headstands.* She was married for eight years to the poet and novelist Jack Marshall and has one son.

POEMS FOR THE NEW

I

we're connecting,
                foot under my rib.
I'm sore with life!
At night,
                your toes grow. Inches of the new!
The lion prowls the sky
and shakes his tail for you.
Pieces of moon
                fly by my kitchen window.
And your father comes
riding the lion's back
                in the dark,
to hold me,
                you,
                    in the perfect circle of him.

2

Voluptuous against him, I am
nothing superfluous,
but all—
bones, bark of him, root of him take.
I am round
with his sprouting,
new thing new thing!
He wraps me.
The sheets are white.
My belly has tracks on it—
                hands and feet
are moving
under this taut skin.
In snow, in light,
we are about to become!

POEM FOR A HUSTLER

Get off my oriental rug, dust I can't shake!
When I hang you out the window and sing
                Good Riddance
you blow
        right
              back
                  in.
Can't you ever just say hello
                without your rug merchant's glasses on
No.
You've got plans.
                Up the middle of you,
                    highways.
And devious country roads
(you think nobody ever heard of)
moving under your fingernails.

I could stare at maps for hours
but you pretend you're not one.
Liar!
      You glitter with the obvious
                glint of a diamond
                on someone's little finger.

I've given you the flowers from my elbows
but it's not enough.
            You're thirsty
            and want straws.
                    No wonder
my veins get nervous when the phone rings!
It might be your tape recorder at the other end
                  taking inventory,
or your milking machine
              and you
disguised in the innocent peasant frills
of a Latvian milkmaid.

Don't you understand there is a sunflower
with an empty horizon
                    in its center
waiting for you to be the dancer?

POEM IN WHICH MY LEGS ARE ACCEPTED

Legs!
How we have suffered each other,
never meeting the standards of magazines
                            or official measurements.

I have hung you from trapezes,
            sat you on wooden rollers,
            pulled and pushed you
                            with the anxiety of taffy,
and still, you are yourselves!

Most obvious imperfection, blight on my fantasy life,
strong,
lump,
never to be skinny
or even hinting of the svelte beauties in history books
                            or Sears catalogues.

Here you are—solid, fleshy and
white as when I first noticed you, sitting on the toilet,
                    spread softly over the wooden seat,
having been with me only twelve years,
                            yet
as obvious as the legs of my thirty-year-old gym teacher.

Legs!
that was the year we did acrobatics
                    in the annual gym show.
How you split for me!
            One-handed cartwheels
            from this end of the gymnasium to the other,
            ending in double splits,

legs you flashed in blue rayon slacks my mother bough
for the occasio
and tho you were confidently swinging along,
the rest of me blushed at the sound of clapping.

Legs!
How I have worried about you, not able to hide you,
embarrassed at beaches, in highschool
when the cheerleaders' slim brown leg
spread all over
the sand
with the perfectic
of bamboo.
I hated you, and still you have never given out on me.

With you
I have risen to the top of blue waves,
with you
I have carried food home as a loving gift
when my arms began u
jelling like madrilenne.
Legs, you are a pillow,
white and plentiful with feathers for his wild head.
You are the endless scenery
behind the tense sinewy elegance of his two dark legs.
You welcome him joyfully
and dance.
And you will be the locks in a new canal between
continent
The ship of life will push out of you
and rejoice
in the whiteness,

in the first floating and rising of wate

LOVE POEM

for Dick

The history of my feeling for you (or is it the way
you change and are blameless like clouds) reminds me

of the sky in Portland and the morning I unpacked and
found the white plates

from Iowa City broken, consistently surprising with cracks,

petals like new math theories smashed with the purposeful
fingers of chance.

I loved the plates. They were remnants from an auction
which still goes on

in my head because of the auctioneer's body and his sexy
insinuations

about the goods he was selling. But to Ruth, who talked
them into their thin wraps

of newspaper, what we were sharing was departure and
two lives breaking

and learning to mend into new forms. We had loved our
husbands, torn

our bodies in classic ways to bear children: Sammy,
Wesley, David—

dearest of what angers and terrifies most. Now we loved
new men and wept

together, so that the plates weren't important and hadn't
been packed

with the care I might have given had I been alone. But
Ruth was with me.

You were gone, like this storm that's been arriving and
disappearing

all morning. I awoke to hear heavy rain in the gutters. The
light was uncertain

and my feelings had grown less sure. Last night, pinned
  by a shaft of pain—
your presence and your absence—I knew clearly that I
  hated you

for entering me profoundly, for taking me inside you to
  the dark place,
for husbanding me, claiming all that I knew and did not
  know, yet letting me

go from you into this unpredictable and loneliest of
  weathers.

9/28/7

DANIELA GIOSEFFI was born of immigrant parents in Orange, New Jersey, 1941. As a child she lived in a Newark ghetto, and later her family moved to a suburb of Paterson. She attended Montclair State Teacher's College, received a B.A. in English and Drama, and then continued studying drama in Washington, D.C., on a scholarship. Her work has appeared in anthologies and her multi-media play, *Care of the Body* (Choice Chapbooks), was produced with a reading of her poems at the Cubiculo Theatre in Manhattan. She received a grant award in 1972 from the New York State Council on the Arts, and she is now living with her daughter Thea in Brooklyn Heights.

301

THE VASES OF WOMBS

—for the Venus of Willendorf

For a long time I've thought about this body of mine
with agony, with curiosity, and the usual dreams
of caressing lovers and children.

For a long time I've thought about these arms
as if they weren't mine but belonged to an Egyptian
       priestess
   raising them over her head to pray or protect the
       hunters
or as though they were handles on the hips of an ancient
       Greek vase
   pedestaled in the still light of the museum.

For a long time I've listened to the blood flowing through
       them
or crossed them over my breasts to imagine rest.
   Some women seem completely unaware of their arms
   wearing them as ornaments without function.

For a long time I've thought about these buttocks,
how they've held me to the earth while others fly
and inhabit the high shelves of libraries.

I've thought about these peering nipples
like the feelers on a cat's face, sensitive to the night.
   Some women pretend not to have them,
   feigning invulnerability.

Men accept mead, soma and nectar from my hands,
blood from my womb, fish from my eyes,
crystals from my eardrums, food from my glands.
In return, they try to pierce the heart
they think ticks between my thighs
pinning me to the bed like a butterfly.

These arms fly out of themselves to talk to you
this head becomes small and sightless
these breasts and buttocks swell
until they are all that is left of me
until I am melted into earth and planted as a garden.

WEARING BREASTS

I sit back in the city
and admire the octopus,
wise old mollusk.
I myself am an ancient fish
wearing new plastic shoes.
My lungs have been through many changes—
breathing first water, then ooze, then air.
Perhaps a tree-climbing fish begat me
and closed the door from youth behind me—
giving me two breasts,
two arms to cuddle children,
and pubic hair
and far too many thoughts for female comfort.

Out of the estuaries
where rivers come again to the sea,
I am a failure of the waters
and can't find my paternal parent
among the creatures that stare from green mud.

PEACE PROSPECT

Too many people scribbling on each others' tongues
gagging the cities.
The politics of the body is muddled by nations.
Sexuality is a force confused, unrealized, and wasted.
Human thoughts have churned up recipes for deadly steel.
sleep awhile

and the marrow of painful earth is played out.
I have a pleasant dream
of a land inhabited only by bright animals
who refuse fire
and eat nothing but leaves.
I count the people I have tried to touch
and my hands melt sand into glass.
There is no chance between us for a fine love.
We can't manufacture food like vegetation
standing in the light.
Photosynthesis is the trees making love with the sun.
A vague intuition blossoms in my stomach.
We are a mind-ridden race and incompatible with earth
A better race will come.
I feel bright animals waiting in my genes
for the right moment.

"WOMAN WITH TONGUE IN CHEEK"

I

There are no rules for so much sadness—
so much despair rising from the sink drains of evening.

The chairs are empty,
the curtains full of wind,
the room complete with silence like a lantern.

Who couldn't talk on—
spilling pages of wordy histories,
cracking thoughts as shells from the nutmeats of philos
     ophies,
spinning threads from the pupils of fish eyes.

2

I lift my breasts waiting for the sky to sprout fingers.
I wait for the calm of an orgasm
but I live in the eye of a hurricane
and can't escape till the clouds burst and the storm end

Men do not let women live in their dreams
but dream of women in their lives
as if we could be as good as trees,
as calm as photosynthesis in all our fornication.

Guilty, guilty, guilty of life,
I pull the trap door shut to close my legs against eternity.
I build a moat around my uterus
and use my ovaries for amulets.
I cease rattling my bracelets.
I cut off my nails.
I pull in my tongue
and close my lips tight
against the kisses of new mournings.

I will not be responsible for temptation.
My hair was not my own idea;
it grew from his rays and he commanded
that I brush it till it shone as moonbeams
because he was the sun,
he was
everyone:

He was Dr. Kildare and Emmett Kelly and Christ,
he was Leonardo da Vinci and Albert Einstein and Louis
    Pasteur,
he was Napoleon and Clark Gable and Allen Planz,
he was Joe Morella and Tony Towle and Wolfgang
    Amadeus Mozart,
he was Norman Pritchard and Plato and Shakespeare,
he was Robert Bly and Ted Hughes and Buddha,
he was Bill Knott, John Logan and Walt Whitman,
he was Jackson Pollock and Allen Ginsberg and Rem-
    brandt,
he was Nathan Whiting and Sam Pullara and Charles
    Nosbaum,
he was Abraham Lincoln and Donato Gioseffi and Richard
    Kearney,
Robert Murch, I have loved you for thirty light years
and I've let you commit crimes in my name!

I've let you force me up onto a pedestal of halos.
I've let you make my hips grow wider
until a child squeezed out of my heart
and grew big as a mountain
and swallowed me for dinner
and held me in its grip until I crooned lullabies.
I've washed a thousand bathtubs
and watered a million geraniums
with the fallings of my dreams
and the knight,
the Knight,
the knight
never comes riding never comes riding
never comes
riding
except to admonish me
for having no mercy
for the politics of his body
or to drape a heavy blue robe around my shoulders
and rest his crucified head
in my big soft and tired lap.

SIV CEDERING FOX was born February 5, 1939 in northern Sweden. She is married and has three children. Her poems have appeared in many little magazines. A tape of her reading in Tokyo with the text will be published in Japan with Japanese translations written and read by George Seito. "River and Light" has been translated into Swedish. She is the recipient of the John Masefield Narrative Poetry Award, 1969; the William Marion Reedy Poetry Award, 1970; and a photography prize from *Saturday Review,* 1970. A special issue of her poetry and photos was published by *Dryad* in the spring of 1971.

RIVER AND LIGHT

I

I sit in the marsh-
light that is golden
from midnight sun,
from tufts,
cotton grass,
cloud berries.

I sit
hunched
behind a dwarfed
pine,

And I see the female moose
and her calf
walk out
into the light
of the marsh.

She lifts her head.
The long ears listen.
The nostrils read
the inhabitants of the wind.

But the wind comes my way.
Undetected
I remain
locked in my human
smell.

And the female moose
and her calf
bend to drink.

The water is rusty with iron
and rainbowed from standing
still between tufts.

The rainbows
stir,
yield to the drinking,
flow in under
velvet nostrils,
to be iron in the hump of the calf,
horn in his crown
and marshlight in the eye of the moose.

I drowse.

A buzzing in my ears
and my eyes open.
I see the head of the cottongrass
letting go,
gathering,
rising,

the spirit of each waterhole
deserting its body
to ghost
over the marsh,
Christ on the churchwall
ascending.

And I drowse,

until an axe
starts to split morning.
I shiver. Rise.
Walk out of the marsh.

2

Once I rode naked on logs
set in their journey

to sawmill
and sea.

I ran out in the water,
caught them in the current,
climbed up and laughed
as they rolled and dunked me
in the river,

to cling, to climb up again,
to float, down-
stream,
arms out, balancing.

And I swam ashore
when I saw the boys
come down to the river,
to strip their clothes off,
to stand, straight as saplings and
slender, hands
hiding genitals, before
that first plunge
into water.

For I had thought about being
that water.
When my body began to curve
like a river,
I loosened my hair and
floated, head first,
the long hair diffusing around me,
strange undulations,
seagrass,
nipples like pebbles.

Soon as wide in the belly
as the river in spring,
swelling,
covering islands and
willows,

I think about death that is only
water
in lungs, fish and gill
floating down-
stream,
the river wide
after thawing.

3

Sweet Christ in the morning!
Is there no ultimate
baptismal?

when your belly carries its own
seas,
where some small being
moves through evolutions?

when you wear your mother's dream
of the white bride
and your father's dream
of the bride of Christ?

When you have been patient
in temporary churches,
tents risen to the new
evangelist: "Come.
Come to Christ. Let Jesus wash . . .
Be purified
in water."

When nothing inside you answered?

I climbed the birchtree,
innocent observer
of bathers and
rowers,
and a white bull was led
and a cow waited,

the cloved monster clumsy on her back,
down,
hit,
hoofs on white hide,
down,
hit,
the long carrot-thing protruding,
up again
and in.

And I climb the stairs
to the abortionist.

4

But the river—

In early spring
the ice tugs at sandbar
and rock.
Blocks tear
loose,
mad with the weight of
winter
and logs
that someone has axed
or screamed electric saws through,
stripped clean of branches,
brought to the river,
trees
slender as boys
and waiting
for ice-break

Stirs,

and I know
it is not to be
the blood of the lamb
but the blood of a woman

when all her rivers let go
and from her own sea
the child comes, the small face
wise as the three kings
and with all
their giving.
And in some room, golden
with morning
and moose-light
something would have to break free.

Daughter, what do I give you?

Christa Fleischmann

LYNN STRONGIN was born in New York City in 1939. She studied musical composition for three years at the Manhattan School of Music, and she received her B.A. from Hunter College and her M.A. from Stanford where she was a Woodrow Wilson Fellow. She moved to California where she taught at Merritt College and Mills College. She says, "I recently realized a long-held dream to move to the desert and am living in Albuquerque where I'm a Teaching Assistant at the University of New Mexico, teaching 'Women in Literature.' " She has made a record with eight other Bay Area poets, *A Day of Poets,* and has had a verse play, *Nocturne,* performed over KPFA, Berkeley. A dance project, *Psalm,* built upon five of her poems, has been choreographed in New York City. Her poetry has been included in several anthologies and she is the recipient of a P.E.N. grant and a grant from the National Institute of Arts and Letters.

READY

eorgia O'Keeffe as a child
ways ate round the raisin in the cookie:
 sought more sky than land in her world,
 t held the jewel at core: renewal
ved best for last.

 recall the black child
 nine or ten, a girl
 who told me with gem-clear eyes
 w her mother'd say, "Always wear clean undies,
 r you never know when you might get hit by a truck."

                              *

hat it amounts to is a scrupulous sense of privacy:
 ere is no way—we can take in every contingency.
 We'd always keep a clean sweep of sky—in mind:
 e'd be prepared, at the same time,
  the loss of it all—the coming clean.

 kely as we are to tread
 the wrong places, like god's little foxes,
 at any time:
 ere is no way we can meet the day with a strong enough
 se of the holy.

VAN GOGH

 s scary the way I am dreaming of flowers
 sessed
 e Van Gogh by the dizzying light of the south.
 ainst February sky
 y marriage looms:
  bear the sleepwalking expression of the weavers;

we lie awake at night with desire;
we think it is the good who are married
who dwell in some visionary south
of innumerable petals

                      pear blossoms

                             irresistible sun.

We stab a potato, snap beans, watch the desert wane
feel shame and know this is our fate
which we must find less bitter than it seems.

Plenitude!
people arguing by a fire, domesticity, a cat . . .
Something gay and tender always comes back.
Just scratch the soil a little in order to get closer
to the source
of the seasons.

                I tear the book open like a hungry ani

                          his bone.

Lights, colors flow in!
I lay back my head, dream
of olive-groves stretching,

                    of the painter who put the l

under the roots
into the leaves that autumn morning . . .

    . . . And, of long black lines of miners going to w

                          in snow

lovers bright, frozen;
the tender glow
of olives in their cheeks would turn
to the fiery red of the mine's inferno.

                Going deeper into earth

                          from southlight

through a shaft
shoulder-to-wheel
yet not hell.

    To come home to a lamp's murkish yellow glow;
    to bend like crude animals, yet gods, over a pla

                            potatoes.

SAYRE

(Woman Professor)

The men in her department envied her.
She was too handsome, had published too many poems.
So, she'd tone down:

she wore olive-drab all that autumn
said she was in a dry season
could not write a single poem.

But her cheeks
took on the flush
of a woman riding.

Hand-to-hip she'd
breathe in the air
of evening.   The casual woman.

Sayre!
She'd claim she was a lonely woman
and besides had a bad spine.   Who'd envy her?

So intense that her fist
would smash glass
a Sunday evening.

But she'd flush a whole nest of quail
out of hiding
without so much as a shotgun   (or a sound.)

Camouflaged
broods of poems came.
The poem for her was—love's occasion.

She'd rise after, with that radiance
of a woman to meet her lover, eye shining
face to face.

Not one of the men guessed it was another woman.
So handsomely she moved, so darkly as through glass

From: FIRST ASPEN

(written for a young woman painter, Alexandra.)

A sensuous Latin poet, now I will go off with a thermos
of coffee, and book of Virgil.
Laughing suddenly, strike a match but the flame's blown

out by desert wind.
Then I hold my head in my hands
with the ridiculous joy of the whole thing:

Young girl, you have made life
joyful again.
(From silence one comes—to it, returns.)

The aspens! each trembling branch
undone
by halo around the young leaves in the year's mature sun

All artists
are aged
in compassion.

I am not so capable of Platonic love as it seems
especially now they are suddenly burning piñon
in New Mexico evenings.

Oh love that *sustains!*
for which I burn: Love that draws the tiredness from,
strong hands on a back, to sleep without pain.

So I turned mean?
said you were young:
It was the earthy gutsy mark of longing:

Salt, the sweat: THE TRUE MARK.
And she will not die whom I loved.   I'm unstrung:
It's dirty luck, that old bird.

But somenight I'l creep up in dark old raincoat
lay hands on you,
and wheeling round you'll suddenly know I seek you.

I'd pass thru dark train windows;
I'd press the monkish curls back from your cheek
molding a statue, instead of hacking poems out of love.

Van Gogh love!
young Russian! What are we to become who are
idealized *even in passion?*

I kiss lips paler than . . .
I touch a forehead in dream, thought springs from.
I hold hands—nervous and young.   First aspen.

This is where sorrow begins.

*

Apology.   Hands shaping air;
holy smell of wood, the mathematical certainty
in your studio-kitchen:

balance of numbers,
beatitude of oil,
steady adding

steady breathing in marriage in your home.
As to mine?   feet moving thru memory.
Life is infinite subtraction:

Oh I can bite the orange rind
well as the next man.
But my palms shine.

I cannot wait till the aspens fall,
leave off being gold,
we may grind them underfoot like crushing out cigarette

Not cry
how we might have held
the cup more to our lips.

Sweetheart there is a brown wind here.
It will sink with the monotony of the passing year.
The words choke in my mouth

as if my hair were blown backward by that wind
which drove you to me,
which drove you to find me.

Neither by my poems nor your art will anyone ever be
quite able to explain our affair.
But it glows in sun (like the little hounds

released from hunt):
It is warm, it is here—
stretched out, relaxed by the fire.

You will rise at night
to brush back your monkish hair,
and perhaps tone down the color of the girl's cheek

in the picture.   I may temper my poem, not so tender.
But today, I would have struck
the first aspen from earth to bring you, in its original flame

Passion—Has it any other name?

*

Sapphic Love!   Sculptress of far more than stone. Alex.
"I love everything about women . . ."
I love to watch water receding from stone, after the storm

leaving the pure form:
Nervous, earthly woman, you are reaching now
to the marrow of my bone.

LYN LIFSHIN grew up in Middlebury, Vermont, where at the age of seven she stole a poem from Blake, and then had to start writing her own poems when people started hearing about this first poem. She says, "I'm still doing a lot of the same things, finding that the poems come true, after I write them." She has given many readings and has published poems in a large number of small magazines and anthologies. Her books of poetry include *Lady Lyn*, Morgan Press; *Why Is the House Dissolving*, Open Skull; *Black Apples*, The Crossing Press; *Leaves and Night Things*, Baby John Press; *Femina 2*, Abraxus; *Tentacles, Leaves*, Helleric; *Moving By Touch*, Cotyledon Press; *Museum*, November Press; *Mercurochrome Sun Poems*, Charis Press; *I'd Be Jeanne Moreau*, Morgan Press; *The Blue Cabin and Other Winter Fruit*, Helleric; *Collected Poems*, The Crossing Press; *Poems*, Northstone Review; and *Love Poems*, Zahir Press.

YOU UNDERSTAND THE REQUIREMENTS

We are
sorry to have to
regret to
tell you
sorry sorry
regret sorry that you have
failed

your hair should have been
piled up higher

you have failed to
pass failed
your sorry
regret your
final hair comprehensive
exam satisfactorily
you understand the requirements

you understand we are
sorry final

and didn't look as professional
as desirable
or sorry dignified
and have little enough
sympathy for 16th century
sorry english anglicanism

we don't know doctoral
competency what to think and
regret you will sorry not
be able to stay
or finish

final regret your disappointment
the unsuccessfully completed best
wishes for the future
it has been a
regret sorry the requirements
the university policy
     please don't call us.

ON THE NEW ROAD

red sumac presses
against the windshield,
tires moan

Your wife dreams
you are guilty,

I button and unbutton
what I feel

From: WALKING THRU AUDLEY END
MANSION LATE AFTERNOON
AND DRIFTING
INTO CERTAIN FACES

down the hall a bookcase
of musty leather

birds of scotland, british
birds, birds of sussex
surrey   devon   the
print fading

some man running ran his
thumb over the page
maybe   his

woman twisting in
chill sheets

who ten years before
listened with him
to the horses in the
leaves   quilt smelling
of skin   flowers

who is rubbing her
hands near the fire
now   letting what
they're full of

rise thru the
chimney into the fog

*   *   *

in some places the color
stayed in the carpets

but these worn places

who walked back and
forth more than
was natural

carrying a sick
child or waiting

rumors of war
in a diary

these mirrors give
nothing back now

*   *   *

stuffed birds in a
cage   in a
glass case pistols
carved bones

is this the
same man who
had all those books

ivory face pasted in a
box   gold writing
in the shadow   gold
coins   4 stone
eggs: his studio

does this have
anything to do
with why his
wife is holding
a lute like an axe

                    *   *   *

why her bedroom is a
trip someplace else

her world of peacocks
snakes and jade trees

she could go any
where with this
box made of ebony

elephants on the
lid   turkish castles

lions   roses   bees

the top still shiny

and the crystal

While he was
stoned on   touched

claws and guns

(no breasts eaten no
mouth on her nipples
not his fingers)

she must have felt like
something under glass
too   candles

dripping all night

green thread flowers
curling under her
cold thighs

her dreams of
black limes, war

SNAKE DANCE

i rub the one bullet
i've ever held against

my lips   put on his
old confederate jacket

we eat hardtack covered
with gold vermillion

High on an iroquois
spell we make each

other tremble　　(i could
be doing that snake

dance　　knowing about
things that bite and

what happens later　　still
taking them into my mouth)

ARIZONA RUINS

I

Past Mogollon River
　　　　　　the limestone ruins
scrape it with your finger
　　　　　　　and the floor breaks
　　　　　　　　　the talc
　　　　　　　must have dusted
　　　　　　　their dark
　　bodies as they squatted on these
　　　　　　　floors grinding
　　　　　mesquite and creosote

No one knows
　　　　　　　　where they went
　　　　　　　from the cliffs
　　with their
　　　　　　earthjars and sandals

　Or if they
cursed the
　　　desert moon
　　　　　　　　as they wrapped
　　their dead
　　babies
　　　　　　in bright cloth
　　　　　　　　and jewels

2

Now cliff swallows
        nest in the mud
      where the Sinaqua
          lived
        until water ran out

High in these white cliffs
          weaving yucca and cotton

    How many nights did they
        listen for cougar
as they pressed the wet
        rust clay
          into bowls

    that they walked
200 miles to trade in Phoenix
    before it was time to leave

        40 years
        before Columbus

3

Noon in the
caves

    it is summer the
        children are sleeping

The women
    listen to a story
    one of them has heard
    of an ocean

        deerflesh dries in the sun

                    they braid
        willow stems
and don't look up

when she
is done
        they are all
stoned on what could come

                                from such water

It is cool and dark
inside here

                this was the place

                        4

The others
have gone to find
salt and red
                stones for earrings

                                the children
                            climb down to
                    look for lizards
                and nuts he

        fucks the girl he
wants
        for the first time

                        her blood cakes
                            on the white chalky floor

                her thighs
                        will make a bracelet
                            in his head

5

Desert bees
         fall thru the wind
     over the pueblos
         velvet ash and barberry

They still find
         bodies
     buried in the wall
         a child's bones
     wrapped in yucca leaves
             and cotton

bats fly thru the
     ruins now
         scrape the charred
     walls white

         the people left
     the debris of their lives here
         arrows, dung
             and were buried
         with the bright
     turquoise they loved
sometimes carved
         into animals and birds

TENTACLES, LEAVES

     he saw my
     picture in a
     magazine and told
     me he wanted
     to take me down

the mississippi
hollering poems and
blowing weed, he
sounded crazy
and i wrote that i'd
never been
beaten   that i was
a bitch too

he sent me
pain and lust
for 19 days   his
aloneness   how he
wanted to fall
into blue water
he said my letters
fell apart
pressed to his
skin   in march
my arms started
melting and

i drank the
chateau ausone
he sent   by april
my face was
burning   he sent
me his so that in
concord i could
just think about
him while the
river was
swelling

but i didn't
think he'd
come   writing bad
checks   stealing
hamburg   staggering

with a torn
suitcase and broken
shoes from california
i didn't know where
to keep him

and got stoned on
cognac before he
fell thru the
door

he taught me to
come and what
men did in
prison   his
eyes weren't mean
and blue
when he said how
we'd live in a
house of shells in
the ferns in
big sur
high on poems
he said we'd eat the
colors off point
lobos   dark
wine and succulents in
bed i could
hear the
seals afternoons
we lay in a blur
of nutmeg
watching the curtains

his head on my
belly telling me about
the women who
stopped mattering

that's when it
started getting
scary   one
waited 5 years after
getting a short
letter

i wouldn't even
take the bus
across town
tho i dreamed i'd go
with him
to yugoslavia
or mexico

he kept getting busted
and moved under the
stairs with
dead moths
drinking beer
and not coughing
then he moved
out into
trees

came leaf by
leaf in the morning

fog was what we
needed   a blur to
lie down and
lie in   i
never liked his
poems as
much as i
pretended   not
even the ones
he stole

but loved the
stories   how he
made love in
coffins   stood
on the roof of his
house screaming
at stars

but he kept
breaking into
places   once
i held him
4 hours while
he cried

next morning he
poured chocolate
in my cunt
and ate it and
talked about
going to montana

we could live in a
wooden hut in
canada with my cats

only nothing was
getting better
he vomited blood
and black things
if he came in
late i thought
it was over

he'd just laugh
we'd take a bottle
out into the
huge weeds
and collapse
laughing

others things fell
too   leaves
he'd slam into
chairs with
cigarettes   burn
holes in everything

i set the clock
ahead   wondered
how long this could
go on   the snow
coming and i

watered the mail
when he went to
get better

and didn't
by october i
couldn't move
wherever i went
there were
tentacles   his
eyes in the
window

i tripped on his
arms and then
cut out for colorado

he couldn't just
stay in the
leaves   children
said he smelled
like fire

lady bugs lie on
their backs now   the
wind is rising

i'm not
sorry that he
came

or that nothing
could keep him

Peter Trump

ERICA JONG was born Erica Mann in New York City, March 26, 1942 (Aries). She studied at Barnard, Columbia Graduate Faculties and Columbia School of the Arts and from 1966 to 1969 she lived in Heidelberg, Germany. Her first book of poems, *Fruits & Vegetables,* was published by Holt, Rinehart and Winston in 1971, and they published her second book, *Half-Lives,* in 1973. She received *Poetry*'s Bess Hokin Prize and also a grant from the New York State Council on the Arts in 1971. She has read at various schools in New York state, at a women's prison, in parks and city squares in New York City, as well as at a Feminist Arts Festival in Buffalo. She says of herself, "Am a happily married feminist and very interested in the power of poetry to liberate women from old self-destructive patterns. And also to liberate men. Amen." Her best-selling novel, *Fear of Flying,* was published in 1974.

ALCESTIS ON THE POETRY CIRCUIT

(In Memoriam *Marina Tsvetaeva, Anna Wickham,
Sylvia Plath, Shakespeare's sister, etc. etc.*)

The best slave
does not need to be beaten.
She beats herself.

Not with a leather whip,
or with sticks or twigs,
not with a blackjack
or a billyclub,
but with the fine whip
of her own tongue
& the subtle beating
of her mind
against her mind.

For who can hate her half so well
as she hates herself?
& who can match the finesse
of her self-abuse?

Years of training
are required for this.
Twenty years
of subtle self-indulgence,
self-denial;
until the subject
thinks herself a queen
& yet a beggar—
both at the same time.

She should mistrust herself
in everything but love.

She should choose passionately
& badly.
She should feel lost as a dog
without her master.
She should refer all moral questions
to her mirror.
She should fall in love with a cossack
or a poet.

She must never go out of the house
unless veiled in paint.
She must wear tight shoes
so she always remembers her bondage.
She must never forget
she is rooted in the ground.

Though she is quick to learn
& admittedly clever,
her natural doubt of herself
should make her so weak
that she dabbles brilliantly
in half a dozen talents
& thus embellishes
but does not change
our life.

If she's an artist
& comes close to genius,
the very fact of her gift
should cause her such pain
that she will take her own life
rather than best us.

& after she dies, we will cry
& make her a saint.

BACK TO AFRICA

"Among the Gallas, when a woman grows tired of the cares of housekeeping, she begins to talk incoherently and demean herself extravagantly. This is a sign of the descent of the holy spirit Callo upon her. Immediately, her husband prostrates himself and adores her; she ceases to bear the humble title of wife and is called 'Lord'; domestic duties have no further claim on her, and her will is a divine law."

—Sir James George Frazer, *The Golden Bough*

Seeing me weary
      of patching the thatch
      of pounding the bread
      of pacing the floor nightly
      with the baby in my arms,

my tall black husband
      (with eyes like coconuts)
      has fallen down on the floor to adore me!
      I curse myself for being born a woman.
      He thinks I'm God!

I mutter incoherently of Friedan, Millet, Greer . . .
      He thinks the spirit
      has descended.
      He calls me "Lord."

*

Lord, lord, he's weary in his castle now.
      It's no fun living with a God.
      He rocks the baby, patches the thatch
      & pounds the bread.
      I stay out all night with the Spirit.

Towards morning when the Spirit brings me home,
      he's almost too pooped to adore me.

I lecture him on the nature
& duties of men.
"Biology is destiny," I say.

Already I hear stirrings of dissent.
He says he could have been a movie star.
He says he needs a full-time maid.
He says he never *meant*
to marry God.

TOUCH

A man in armor,
a huge plume
shooting from his head,
velvet buckles at his hips,
joints of oiled steel
moving with the sound
of taffeta,
comes to my room
late at night.

His face is visored.
His chest
is emblazoned with crowns.
A fine tattoo of gold
blooms on his arms.

Through a chink in the visor
I see what may be an eye,
or perhaps the reflection
of its loss.

His codpiece gleams like a knife.

I think myself naked,
my skin white

as the cut side of a pear.
I think he will slash me.

But when we move
our bodies together
we make such noises . . .

It has been this way for years.
Our steel hands clasp.
Our legs lock into place
like coupling freight trains.

HOOK

Nights we spend apart
 am at the bottom of a lake
with my loneliness.
Even a fishhook
would taste good.
 throw myself a line.
 write.

Night terrors come back.
 am four.
There is a man under the bed
who holds his breath
so I will think he's dead.
 know he's cheating
 I hold mine too.
We wait each other out.

Last gasp.
The water fills my lungs.
WOMAN KILLED BY DROWNING IN HER DREAMS.

At the bottom of the world
where books dissolve,
then pencils turn to salt,

where Venice sinks
under the weight
of stolen gold,
the blind fish bump me
& I turn to them.

I speak their silent thoughts
before I sleep.

SEMINAR

They are the clean boys from the midwest
who come to New York
with pennies on their tongues
to pay the piper.

They open their mouths & money tumbles out
this ought to be
negotiable for poems
but it is not.

Oh they are glib as pockets full of change
& all have girlfriends
& all turn on
& all get laid two times a week, at least,
& write about it.

They bring their poems to the man
who's slept with death,
& are baffled
when he laughs.

WHY I DIED

She is the woman I follow.
Whenever I enter a room
she has been there

    with her hair smelling of lions & tigers,
    with her dress blacker than octopus ink,
    with her shoes moving like lizards
    over the waving wheat of the rug.

Sometimes I think of her as my mother
but she died by her own hand
before I was born.

    She drowned in the waves of her own hair.
    She strangled on Isadora's scarf.
    She suckled a poisonous snake at her breast
    like Cleopatra or Eve.

She is no virgin & no madonna.
Her eyelids are purple.
She sleeps around.

    Wherever I go I meet her lovers.
    Wherever I go I hear their stories.
    Wherever I go they tell me,
    different versions of her suicide.

I sleep with them in gratitude.
I sleep with them to make them tell.
I sleep with them as punishment or reward.

    She is the woman I follow.
    I wear her cast-off clothes.
    She is my mother, my daughter.
    She is writing this suicide note.

BITTER PILLS FOR THE DARK LADIES

"—hardly a person at all, or a woman,
certainly not another 'poetess,' but . . ."
—Robert Lowell about Sylvia Plath

If you've got to   if after trying to
give it up (like smoking or Nembutal)
if after swearing to   shut it up   it keeps on
yakking (that voice in your head)
that insomniac who lives across the wall,
that amateur Hammondist
who plays those broken scales next door
o then   consider yourself doomed to.

Ambition bites. Bite back.
(It's almost useless.) Suppose yourself born
half black, half Jewish in Mississippi, & with one leg
                    You get the Idear?
Jus' remember you got no rights. Anything go wrong
they gonna roun' you up & howl "Poetess!"
(sorta like "Nigra!") then kick the shit outa you
sayin': You got Natural Rhythm (28 days)
so why you wanna mess aroun'?

Words bein' slippery & poetry bein'
mos'ly a matter of balls,
men what gives in to the lilt and lift of words
(o love   o death   o organ tones   o dickey!)
is "Cosmic." You is "Sentimental."
So dance in your Master's bed (or thesis) & shut
yo' mouth. Ain't you happiest there?

If they let you out   it's as Supermansaint
played by S. Poitier   with Ph.D.[2]   & a buttondown

washed whiter than any other on the block.
& the ultimate praise is always a question of nots:

> viz. not like a woman
> viz. "certainly not another 'poetess' "

meanin'

> she got a cunt but she don't talk funny
> & he's a nigger but he don't smell funny

& the only good poetess is a dead.

SUMMER BRENNER, born in 1945, grew up in Atlanta, Georgia, and went to school in Atlanta and Boston with a two-year interim in Europe—"all of which," she says, "is very important on rainy days." She now lives in New Mexico, which she considers home, and helped edit *Best Friends* in Albuquerque. She says of herself, "I drive a 1948 Dodge, love puppets, and make good soup." Her book of poems, *Everyone Came Dressed As Water*, will be published by the Grasshopper Press.

DEDE'S RETURN TO NEW MEXICO

Sometimes we meet like old lovers
or mother and child
letting what is subdued and sad
settle on us like smoke
will go away
like a river that is gray now
vague like the color of leaves now
it is November

The sky is evenly blue today
I do not believe in horizon
I see without dissolution
the resistance of limb to blue air

When many things in each house
were almost intolerable
when we were friends
when our hands shredded the edges and made them into
    lace
Now part of us is older
and the past constructs a stone heart
Rather let our livers strait the poisons out

The grasses are the color of bleach
Left by the water are a few green weeds
This will be the winter I learn to smell

My smile is a little unctuous
I am willing to please
Yours is less than generous
One of us should be more stupid

The green of this time is passive
I am glad you are with your lover
He knows where to hold you
You know where to be strong with him
Your past recalls a self-control

My arms are all askew
They clumsily push your tears to the blue edges
They finger words in air that are too bold
Soon I will fold them away

FOR PAIGE

All Sunday I sat as lady
with dress and slip
and apron for sauce
I featured myself quiet
with the echoes of a house
alone at work

I thought this man does love me so
especially as lady
standing in winter skirts
impervious to the nature of my body
ignorant of its dance
he loves me so
aloof from lustful glances
caring for brandy and cold

He fears for me in summer
too naked and too brown
I am brash with the sun
I am brash with my lover
The winter's moon is pale and shy
in faded denim and heavy socks
The rage of cold is silent
Its kisses stick to the tongue
and its body hides behind wilting breasts
The sun is womb-bold
It outrages the roofs
he fears for me—he loves me so

May I

*

Mother, they say you looked Irish
hair black as gypsy
eyes blue as an Andalusian doll
Mother, do you want some water?
Mother, do you want some light?

Mother, I saw you lying on a bed
You were a form of solid shadows
The substance was your laugh hiding in a drawer
Mother, I believe you're dying

There are attic trunks around
open and strewn with odd and old
things of a century before
another mother time in death
in France—perhaps Bretagne
where grey old moss wrought things persist
and the land is pierced from time to time
with a glance from a Gaelic blue eye

Mother, do you want some water?
Mother, do you want some light?
Twice now I have cried in a dream of your death
I failed to hear the laughter
It tinks against the glass now

Mother, there is an old photograph
of a farmhouse
two story on the Plains
One of the windows upstairs is open
I slipped in and found you here
It was good to be by you
Mother, they say you were beautiful

1970

Isabel Mardiat

SHARON BARBA was born in Ohio in November of 1943. She is currently writing a feminist study of Willa Cather for her Ph.D. dissertation at the University of New Mexico, where she has taught women's literature courses in the freshman English program. A member of Women's Liberation and the Best Friends women's poetry collective in Albuquerque, she has published poems in little magazines and feminist periodicals.

LETTER REACHING OUT
TO MY SISTER, 1600 MILES

I cannot think of you
apart from your men
All those years
you were potential   for them

for a husband locked in
by government men
You will be his woman-waiting
writing long letters no doubt
reminding him   there will be
trees on the farm   & water
& love is the thing which holds together

& tell him of his son
the current that runs between you
the way he is learning his name
& how to stand up

I wished you a daughter
tho it was your baby after all
& you were glad for a boy
ignoring the bad delivery
ignoring the pain   since you
loved him before he was born
loved him before he was conceived
loved him before you found
the father to make him

If the same mother made us
she is as dual as we are
she contains us both
Once she said she should have been a nun
(not knowing how else to say it)
but she had to get us born
daughter of love & daughter of bitterness
daughter of men & daughter of women

daughter of children & daughter who
holds her womb hostage against them

I knew you all the time   you say
I saw your wounding   how you
hold yourself into yourself
You hoped he would heal me
seeing no other hope   and when
I wrote   saying I'd left him
you said only   You make things so
difficult   you always have
you could have loved him simply

We are sisters
we are the halves of woman
Someday we will be healed
& made whole
& our daughters will not
distinguish between us

THANKSGIVING

The beauty of
          the male face
acknowledging sorrow
of a man who hurts
and lets you see

I had almost forgotten
               my brothers
when you cried
I had almost
               learned to hate
when your face changed

In that room the air
          stopped being frozen

words stopped
        banging together
and I
        began to move

I never thought
            it would be a man
I thought women were alone
that your hands were
            like steel
until I held on to them

until you closed your eyes
and grief like
            red glass
                illumined you
and I could see again
with doubled vision

Nov. 27, 1971

DROPPING
TOWARD STILLNESS

Her mind is a stone   dull
and smooth at the edges

Even the voices she loves
sound strange   and muffled
passing through phones
and long-distance handkerchiefs

There are people who say
they know her   attendants
who fix the wires   and believe
that shock is therapeutic

that the first principle
is to keep moving   to stay
awake   not to go mute

Inside it gets quieter
and the secret box she lives in
makes motion harder

She means to tell them that
but the words latch in
Her throat is shutting down

A CYCLE OF WOMEN

It is that dream world Anaïs speaks of
that dark watery place
where everything is female
where you open the door of the house
and she waits upstairs
the way you knew she would
and her hair floats over the world

Every woman has a history
mother and grandmother and the ones before that
the faces she sees in dreams or visions
and wonders *Who?* A childless woman
waking at night to the hard pull, the old
contractions, the birth cry of her mothers.
Or the heaviness in her back from stooping,
her hips from iron belts, the lines in
her face from mountain women.

Or, longer ago than that, the spears
and battleaxes, that ache in the thighs
from straining tight on the horses.
And the old queens, before history began,
when it was her story they told,
did they wrap their heads in bright cloth,

wear bracelets? or were they nude
and savage, their breasts large and
firm, their feet solid on their solid earth?

Each one is queen, mother, huntress
though each remembers little of it
and some remember nothing at all,
resting in crazy houses
from the long spin of history
drinking the grief of their sex
eating it in bitter pills
muttering in kitchens,
telling their daughters
the story of a sleeping princess
but knowing it takes more than a man's kiss
to wake one so bent on sleeping her life away:

someone who should be kept in an ice-box
until she is ready; then wake her up, as now,
into a cave or a field,
using perhaps the kiss of a sister.
Let her go from there, start over,
live it again, until she knows who she is.
Until she rises as though from the sea
not on the half-shell this time
nothing to laugh at
and not as delicate as he imagined her:
a woman big-hipped, beautiful, and fierce.

NIKKI GIOVANNI comes from the Black city of Lincoln Heights, Ohio. At sixteen she entered Fisk University where she studied writing with John Killens and edited the campus literary magazine. On returning to Cincinnati, she initiated an awareness of arts and culture in the Black community, beginning with the first Cincinnati Black Festival in 1967 and the establishment of the New Theatre. Her books are *Black Feeling, Black Talk, Black Judgment; Gemini; Re: Creation;* and *Night Comes Softly*. She is now living in New York and is on the staff of Rutgers' Livingston College.

SEDUCTION

one day
you gonna walk in this house
and i'm gonna have on a long African
gown
you'll sit down and say "The Black . . ."
and i'm gonna take one arm out
then you—not noticing me at all—will say "What about
this brother . . ."
and i'm going to be slipping it over my head
and you'll rapp on about "The revolution . . ."
while i rest your hand against my stomach
you'll go on—as you always do—saying
"I just can't dig . . ."
while i'm moving your hand up and down
and i'll be taking your dashiki off
then you'll say "What we really need . . ."
and i'll be licking your arm
and "The way I see it we ought to . . ."
and unbuckling your pants
"And what about the situation . . ."
and taking your shorts off
then you'll notice
your state of undress
and knowing you you'll just say
"Nikki,
isn't this counterrevolutionary . . . ?"

NIKKI-ROSA

childhood remembrances are always a drag
if you're Black
you always remember things like living in Woodlawn
with no inside toilet
and if you become famous or something
they never talk about how happy you were to have

your mother
all to yourself and
how good the water felt when you got your bath
from one of those
big tubs that folk in chicago barbecue in
and somehow when you talk about home
it never gets across how much you
understood their feelings
as the whole family attended meetings about Hollydale
and even though you remember
your biographers never understand
your father's pain as he sells his stock
and another dream goes
And though you're poor it isn't poverty that
concerns you
and though they fought a lot
it isn't your father's drinking that makes any difference
but only that everybody is together and you
and your sister have happy birthdays and very good
Christmasses
and I really hope no white person ever has cause
to write about me
because they never understand
Black love is Black wealth and they'll
probably talk about my hard childhood
and never understand that
all the while I was quite happy

FOR SAUNDRA

i wanted to write
a poem
that rhymes
but revolution doesn't lend
itself to be-bopping

then my neighbor
who thinks i hate

asked—do you ever write
tree poems—i like trees
so i thought
i'll write a beautiful green tree poem
peeked from my window
to check the image
noticed the school yard was covered
with asphalt
no green—no trees grow
in manhattan

then, well, i thought the sky
i'll do a big blue sky poem
but all the clouds have winged
low since no-Dick was elected

so i thought again
and it occurred to me
maybe i shouldn't write
at all
but clean my gun
and check my kerosene supply

perhaps these are not poetic
times
at all

Ruth Rosen

SUSAN GRIFFIN was born in 1943. She is a college graduate, an unemployed former waitress, teletypist, proofreader, and teacher. Divorced. She now lives in Berkeley with women who are sharing the attention of her three-year-old daughter. She is writing a novel slowly, poems quickly, and journalism under pain of hunger. Shameless Hussy Press published her first book of poems, *Dear Sky*. She has been published in *Ramparts, Aphra, Remember Our Fire III, Off Our Backs, Ain't I a Woman, The Tribe,* and *The Guardian.* Her second book of poems, *Journey into a Troubled Freedom,* is unpublished. She won the Ina Coobbrith Award in 1963, but remained unpublished until women began to print women.

Love should grow up like a wild iris in the fields,
unexpected, after a terrible storm, opening a purple
mouth to the rain, with not a thought to the future,
ignorant of the grass and the graveyard of leaves
around, forgetting its own beginning. Love should
grow like a wild iris
but does not.
Love more often is to be found in kitchens at the dinner
        hour,
tired out and hungry, lingers over tables in houses where
the walls record movements; while the cook is probably
        angry,
and the ingredients of the meal are budgeted, while some
where a child cries feed me now and her mother not quite
hysterical says over and over, wait just a bit, just a bit,
love should grow up in the fields like a wild iris
but never does
really startle anyone, was to be expected, was to be
predicted, is almost absurd, goes on from day to day, not
        quite
blindly, gets taken to the cleaners every fall, sings old
songs over and over, and falls on the same piece of rug that
never gets tacked down, gives up, wants to hide, is not
brave, knows too much, is not like a
wild iris growing wild but more like
someone staring into space
in the street
not quite sure
which door it was, annoyed about the sidewalk being
slippery, trying all the doors, thinking
if love wished the world to be well, it would,
love should
grow up like a wild iris, but doesn't, it comes from
the midst of everything else, sees like the iris

of an eye, when the light is right,
feels in blindness and when there is nothing else is
tender, blinks, and opens
face up to the skies.

April, 71

REVOLUTION

I would not have gotten in this boat with you.
I would not
except
where else was there
at the docks end
to go?
the water
was cold.

I would not have let you row the boat.
I could see
what kind of man you were.
I would not except
who was there to choose
between
you and me?

I would not have let you throw away the oars.
I knew what would happen next.
except
what else was there to do,
struggle
in a boat with a leak
over cold water?

THE SKY

You said
We will all
have to
be the sky.
(we had just crawled
through dark places.)
oh, and it *is*
counter-revolution,
she said it,
to despair.
I wanted to die
and in the next moment
to go to Europe,
to sit atrophied
at a table with sweet coffee
or walk past red walls
and stare
into the ruins, just like a
soldier marbelized into
eternal surprise. We
must
live daily lives,
(we do anyway) and still
fall to the depth
of whatever in us wants
to fly apart as water
flys apart and apart
in waves, yet there is
no way
to fall and still
save what we want
to come back for,
we hold
one another:
but *we* cannot wait
despair works against us
and so does pain

that is suicidal or
homicidal;
shall I kill myself
or you? we cannot
wait, we cannot
turn away again
saying, "my children and their children
will carry on," when we
cannot carry on ourselves,
it seems, one more day.
To say, "tomorrow,"
is to deny
our living selves
and now the sun plays
in too real a way
against your faces, I love
you both. we are
sitting together in January grass, there is
no denying the greenness around us,

make it so.
the children
will be loved
make that so, and the children
in us, loved again
what makes my heart
                    open
                         one
                              day

then closed, then grieve
again and again   is the same with us all.
this is so and shall I
apologize that there is
only
so much I can
bear, all women
can bear?
We who are sitting
on life and being

told how
by death must
stop listening,
and hear again
what we
want, we are
the sky.

I LIKE TO THINK OF
HARRIET TUBMAN

I like to think of Harriet Tubman.
Harriet Tubman who carried a revolver,
who had a scar on her head from a rock thrown
by a slave-master (because she
talked back), and who
had a ransom on her head
of thousands of dollars and who
was never caught, and who
had no use for the law
when the law was wrong,
who defied the law. I like
to think of her.
I like to think of her especially
when I think of the problem of
feeding children.

The legal answer
to the problem of feeding children
is ten free lunches every month,
being equal, in the child's real life,
to eating lunch every other day.
Monday but not Tuesday.
I like to think of the President
eating lunch Monday, but not
Tuesday.
And when I think of the President

and the law, and the problem of
feeding children, I like to
think of Harriet Tubman
and her revolver.

And then sometimes
I think of the President
and other men,
men who practise the law,
who revere the law,
who make the law,
who enforce the law
who live behind
and operate through
and feed themselves
at the expense of
starving children
because of the law,
men who sit in paneled offices
and think about vacations
and tell women
whose care it is
to feed children
not to be hysterical
not to be hysterical as in the word
hysterikos, the greek for
womb suffering,
not to suffer in their
wombs,
not to care,
not to bother the men
because they want to think
of other things
and do not want
to take the women seriously.
I want them
to take women seriously.
I want them to think about Harriet Tubman,
and remember,
remember she was beat by a white man

and she lived
and she lived to redress her grievances,
and she lived in swamps
and wore the clothes of a man
bringing hundreds of fugitives from
slavery, and was never caught,
and led an army,
and won a battle,
and defied the laws
because the laws were wrong, I want men
to take us seriously.
I am tired, wanting them to think
about right and wrong.
I want them to fear.
I want them to feel fear now
as I have felt suffering in the womb, and
I want them
to know
that there is always a time
there is always a time to make right
what is wrong,
there is always a time
for retribution
and that time
is beginning.

Henry Carlile

SANDRA McPHERSON was born in San Jose, California, August 2, 1943. She received her B.A. in English from San Jose State College and did work toward an M.A. in writing at the University of Washington. She has worked as a technical writer, and has been guest editor for *Poetry Northwest*. She has been anthologized in *American Literary Anthology III* and *Best Poems of 1968*. Her first book, *Elegies for the Hot Season,* was published by Indiana University Press in 1970 and was selected by the National Council on the Arts for a program designed to aid university presses. She also received the Helen Bullis Prize from *Poetry Northwest* in 1968. She now lives in Portland, Oregon with her husband and her daughter Phoebe who is the author of two one-line poems to appear in Duane Ackerson's *Dragonfly* anthology of one-line poems.

THREE FROM THE MARKET

I

Come, radishes, rosy against your greens,
crisp when I am soft with weakness.

Oh what voluptuaries you are! yet
with the definitive sharpness of the scissors.

Ambition dances about you,
yet you are totally unmoved, like true

emissaries of red.

I, what there is of me, may be argued:
but you may not.   Your whole self struts;
your leafiness flutters above your head
like a crown of doves.

No radish was ever terrified.

How you cheer me, strong souls for a dime.

2

I count 12 sections
nearly always, or average,
and buy Coachella grapefruit just to tabulate
12 until my refrigerator rolls with them
like model atoms
whose number is 12.

That's magnesium
of the intense white light.
Grapefruit's white energetic light
befits it as a morning dish.
Count 12 in the morning
and half the day is light.

But have you seen them grow
in the mineral white deserts?
More light more light.
This is the composition of grapefruit:
34% rind, membrane, seeds;
the rest is light.

3

O sad grapes,
sad as Chavez's eyes,
weighted with the very press
of holy tradition,

if I used to savor
even your rotting ones,
each with a different phase
of flavor

like waning moons,
you'll have to pardon me.
I must have known in my dreams
of the coming, voluntary

famine.
They say GI's have developed
a sudden taste for you,
O innocents.

But I imagine you on my table,
green on it, fresh and new.
Someday you will not need to bring with you
the knowledge of good and evil.

HOLDING PATTERN

for Sister Madeline DeFrees
and Sister Michele Birch

Poetry is a way of counting,
                sisters,
                        it is acquisitive.
I try to find something to hold on to,
                        laid up in heaven.
Held down,
        ill at ease,
                but blameless,
                        I meet no one in the air,
In terrible anticipation to walk
                with you,
                    paper-soled
Women,
        into the brick learning places
                    and open-windowed rooms.
So it is eternal—
            this aught
                that we believe to be a high
Degree of order
        with the controlled
                suspense of the sun.
As I circle you
        you hold your crosses
                sacred, those four
Straight routes
        that draw off pain
                and that lightning
Body they ground.
        I began with a line
                hardly a pardonable
Sin in my book.
        How much should you see
                of yourself,
                    or say?

Sometimes I want to be told
    what is great.
       "We have developed
A slight technical difficulty
     and may not be able to land
Without a mechanic."
    We are in the habit of writing,
         and any
Power
  we may derive from each other's company
       will circle quietly
Over the page,
    complicated as what we don't see
       but the pilot knows.
In whatever space
    we fly by our own mettle
       with words that count
Much as friends
    and with a heightened sense
       of where it all ends.

A GIFT OF TRILLIUMS

Bandage-white and healthy
Illegally they came
From their wild bed in the ferns
To our back door. You saw them
Far off and ran
To dig your fingers around roots
Frailer than baby hands,
To baby the two heads.
Siamese on one root, home
To this human mother.

Nurse, the spade!—the kitchen
Spoon. Our first transplant
Flops completely: one stalk's
A collapsing lung, the other,

Face in the mud, prays
For our disgrace.
They are just out of breath.
They need an Easter and lo,
Three days healing, they do
Spring back, show
Their napkin-white faces,
Come blushing into being.

It is their new life which is
Your gift, not their old wood-
Wild prettiness
And privacy: this new
Prosperity they shout like lepers
Lucky to be healed.
Among the snow-browned shrubs and
Dandelions of our rented garden
These trilliums stun
Like nudes, though you knew
Not how they would bless when you
Thieved them nor did I know
How like our flesh they would become.

ELEGIES FOR
THE HOT SEASON

1. *The Killing of the Snails*

Half the year has hot nights, like this,
When gnats fly thick as stars, when the temperature is
    taken
On the tongues of flowers and lovers,
When the just-dead is buried in warm sod.
The snail-pebbled lawns glimmer with slime trails, and the
    unworried,
Unhurried snail tucks into his dark knuckle, stockaded
With spears of grass, safe.   When I first heard
The sound of his dying, it was like knuckles cracking.

The lightest foot can slay snails.   Their shells break
More easily than mirrors.   And like bad luck, like
A face in a mirror, they always come back.

Good hunting nights were stuffy as a closed room.
No moon shone but my father's flashlight.
As if it were Jericho, he circled the house,
And I'd hear all evening the thick crunch
Of his marching, the sound of death due
To his size 13 shoe.

In the morning I'd find them, little clots on the grass,
     pretend
They'd been singed by geranium fire-bursts, asphyxiated
     by blue
Iris flame, burnt to shadows under the strawberry blossom.
The fuchsias bled for them.   White-throated calla lilies
Maintained appearances above the snail slum.

But the slow-brained pests forgave and fragilely claimed
     the garden
The next hot season, like old friends, or avengers.

2. *The Killing of the Caterpillars*

Today I watch our neighbor celebrating May,
Ringing round the besieged cherry-tree,
His haunted maypole, brandishing his arson's torch
Through the tents of caterpillars.   He plays conductor,
Striking his baton for the May music.
And the soft, fingery caterpillars perform,
Snap, crackle, pop.

They plummet through a holiday of leaves like fireworks or
     shooting stars or votive candles
Or buttercups, under the hex of the neighbor's wand, first
     fruits of euthanasia,
Ripe and red before the cherries.   And it is over,

Grown cold as a sunset. They lie on the grass
Still and black as those who lie under it.

It is night. Lights burn in the city
Like lamps of a search-party, like the search-beam
Of my father's flashlight, at every swing discovering
Death.

Checani

ANNE WALDMAN was born in April, 1945 in Millville, New Jersey, although she grew up in New York City on Macdougal Street. She still lives off and on in New York, directing the Poetry Project at St. Mark's Church in-the-Bowery, where she's been since graduating from Bennington College in 1966. She is the author of three books of poems: *Baby Breakdown*, Bobbs-Merrill, *Giant Night*, Corinth, and *No Hassles*, The Kulchur Foundation. Bobbs-Merrill will publish a new book of poems in 1973. She edits a poetry magazine, *The World*, and she is co-editor of Angel Hair Books. She edited two anthologies, *The World Anthology* and *Another World*, and she won a National Literary Anthology Award for 1970.

TRAVELING

Europe overwhelms me!
Why I've hardly caught my breath

Isn't it strange to be noble in this day and age?
Step one foot inside and you'll camp for life

Not really, but this does remind me of certain landscapes
not compelling or realized
but about to be, then dead forever

But that's not so bad if you've had a good life
and want to stop for the paper first

Want to?

Violence is here, everywhere and in Europe
So I'm warning you to take your heart along

Open it up at the right time like presents
and give it to some violent, deserving soul

Last night, reading the paper, I thought of Shakespeare
Boy did he get around just like the news!

He had the right idea
and it's a good impulse jumping uptown like this
though there aren't any movies
and we're forced to stay "on the move" in our heads

But that's true anywhere at this hour of the morning
which overwhelms me like "breathing"

or knowing enough of the world gets through without me

RESISTING
EACH OTHER

when that happens
your world is split
despair
what to do with these hands?

wait & stare

talk is no answer

it's sunny

hello? hello?
are you there? (no more)

you are half the person
you were
half there

OVER ASIA

A life is suspended over foreign countries
I haven't been to
                    but know they exist
like you might take a walk in your own neighborhood
                        (so much garbage in the streets)
(a blackout)
                to understand war conditions
(One must stay inside, not eat too much, etc.)
Is this happening to me?
                I doubt it will
right now at least
                All the lights in the world in New York Cit

All the books
      People
Every day something new happening
           The mind reaches forward
gets hooked on the horizon
         and just hangs there
watching, studying out the situation with a crazy interest
(and Asia rages miserably below)

ROMANTIC POEM

it's true that days are longer in the country

      but
how nice you are to say so

      Mr. & Mrs. Squirrel

      *

I love the way you take me
      long afterwards I'm still yours

      love becoming love becoming love

HOLY CITY

Because it has sunk so low
like loss, like big loss
Because my heart heaves
in its 26 year old breast
& spirit broken like an arrow
under the immense tear
whose power, sorrow, expands
in all directions all the time

Because it's tired & staked out
& no amends to fill the duty
& no windows to see the result
forget itself & climb down
from a bastion of steel
or slip cautiously from a cake of cement
Because your friends are as distant
as stars from the street
& your lover sighs & goes to sleep
leaving you, the dreamer, to the untender mercy
of the clock, dirty dawn, job,
school report, speeding ticket
all rushing forward
to trip you up
as you sidestep the ledge
& that ledge is a clean line
straight to the end
over & over again
making the same mistake
though you pinpoint it
track it down
& wipe your target clean
They'll still trip you up
Because it's not architecture
or instinct or cultivation
or the last word or the tops
or justice or the right of way
or extra fine quality or cheap
or even reasonable
Because the rain is as classical as ever
the people sleep late & grumble
the traffic stalls & monsters your breath
& money talks & money screams & tortures you
& maniacs grab at your pocketbook
& grope your ass
& the best poet in town packs a gun
Because there's no way
back or out just a tighter & tighter squeeze
with junk to drown your sadness

& junk to wire your madness
Because you feel imminent death all the time
though I'm not afraid no I'm not afraid
Because it's throwing a bright idea straight to hell
& becoming the slow & patient destruction
of all you ever wanted to do.

NYC '71

Mat Hunter

MIRIAM PALMER was born in 1946 (Taurus). She says of herself, "I don't come from anywhere, not sure where I'm going, just write lots of poems, work on Women's Liberation, do odd jobs to make money. I live in Maine because the people are friendly and the air is clean. I went to college and have a degree —but I pretty much ignore it." She put together a book of her poems called *Mothers & Daughters*.

"VIERGE OUVRANTE"

Under her deep plush roof
she is water,
she runs in room after room,
so clear we see through her
like eyes or laughter.
Hers are the simplest desires
made visible
in coiled gold leaves
on picture frames and rococo
angel centerpieces.
She is never ashamed
of the obvious,
of calling her husband "Daddy"
or saying "those people" in conversation.

"Can you imagine how horrible
to wake up and find a black man in bed with you!"

She can't find her son or daughter anywhere,
she calls and calls in her sleep.
In the attic there is nothing but an old flute
and a football.
When her son married
there were no pretences—
she sobbed through each night
to an exhausted morning, and prayed,
really believed
she could save him.
Now her fat,
mother-hollow body
shudders
as she catches his hand
on the girl's light breast,
and she is afraid.

"Oh I can't do anything. It's old age.
I can't even control my hands anymore."

And all her life it's been this endless tide
of pain, of not liking
her husband, children, garden
or even the piano,
of never knowing, only
that it was supposed to be that way.
She rearranges the heavy furniture
Mother gave her
over and over, like a rosary,
and brings each stranger in to see,
to ask them, "Is this the place?"
"Have I found it?"
"May I stop here?"

    "This house is everything to us now,
    we've worked so hard on it!"

But finally they all smile
and have to leave her.
She sits in Mother's rocker
and sinks herself back
to that just-beginning,
that blessed virgin
-ity, when the nuns
made a dresden magic over everything.
Flowers never died
and never bloomed, there were no necessities,
no demands
from husband-children-strangers,
her hands in their purity
never trembled on the keys
and the light
always followed her to mass.

GETTING INTO FOCUS

for Carole

Running your apartment
through my fingers,
sifting
the photographs
and carefully invented
flowers,
dissolving
into your eyes, cut
into a hundred facets
like a fly's.
I find the smells
of delicate teas and powders—
alfalfa, mullein, burdock—
and the trace of lemon-honey
you leave.
The wardrobe
lurches
against the wall,
a purple fantasy shipwreck.
Slender dresses
cling
to a remembrance of richness
like seashells
each holding a drop of perfect
gold oil.   No music,
silence of yoga,
magnetic circles
from room to room, overlapping.
When you return
you will weave it together
in your dark room
the way a fish weaves blue
water with black.
I could be another delighted
victim.

Or I could steal your key,
lock you
into the sky
with your voluptuous white cat,
feed you
on ginseng and honey
from queen bees,
give you
wild strawberry lotion
for your breasts and cunt.
Then I would put on
one of your fragile masks—
the elephant dragon
or the swollen-faced yellow lady
with the crushed nose and cheek—
and dance you
into a sleep for seven days,
into a country with no machines,
no cameras or collages,
where the models would refuse
all distortions, go back
to their bodies of blood
and grass.
And all those faces
you saw in the mirrors
break,
come through
to embrace you
shining
and alone.

Richard Friedman

ANITA BARROWS, born in 1947 in Brooklyn, grew up in Long Island suburbia. She went to various colleges East and West, received a B.A. in creative writing from San Francisco State, and an M.A. in English Literature from Boston University. She has been published in various little magazines, including *Aphra: the feminist literary magazine,* and has won awards from *The Atlantic Monthly* and *New Magazine*. She is the poetry editor for Radio KPFA in Berkeley. She has taught in an experimental school in the Bay Area and developed and taught a writing workshop for high school students. Currently living in a small house surrounded by eucalyptus in the Oakland, California hills, she is teaching, writing and doing French translations.

THE MUTANT

Was this the daughter you bargained for,
a daughter with teeth for an eye?
What kind of prayers do they answer
for mothers in January coats,

for fathers with dovetail hands?
What a loaf to bake in your oven!
What a paycheck!   What a corsage!

The neighbors kept theirs
in a closet, the idiot boy
whose head grew like fungus
from broomstick legs.   But yours—

what could you do with it?
Outside, she devoured everything.
She ate you out of house
and home—everything—

pennies, gingerbread, bone.
What's more, you said you loved her.
Would sell your clothes, sell
your business for her.   The rabbis

you brought her to lowered their heads:
she siphoned their beards like licorice.
The doctors said, operate: Like a rat
she made off with their instruments.

And what an embarrassment she was!
If you brought her to a lake,
she drank it.   If she looked out
the window, the landscape

was stubbled and charred.
The relatives were sympathetic:

naturally she would never marry.
And what would you do

with all that strange digestion?

January, 1970

LETTER TO A FRIEND
IN AN UNKNOWN PLACE

For days I have been walking around
with a great bird tied to my neck.
His claws have taken on the thinness of my veins,
so that both of us are warmed
by the same blood, like trees
whose roots are knotted together beside a river.

He will not tell me who he is, or
what species of bird he belongs to, or
what is the country he comes from.   I
cannot tell, by feeding him,
whether he is life-eater or death-eater,
flower- or fish-eater: Everything

I offer, he refuses.   Still, he is growing.
The first day I called him my brother.
He was as small as my fist, and nested
like a weapon behind my shoulder.   Later, he grew
to the size of my open hand; and his pulse
copied like tape the moon in my wrist.

Also, he has opened his eyes.   I have tried writing down,
with their strange light behind me, all the things
I know about him.   He has no song.
His wings must be bound, like the skin of an orange,
over his breast: there is no sound in his feathers
when the wind moves.   He shows no interest in flying.

May, 1971

FIRE

Somebody's
house is on fire.   Somebody's
furniture is dancing, a swarm
of yellow bees.   Somebody's kitchen
table hisses and glows
in the broken windows.   Somebody's
portraits are pinned
to the wall, and exploding
like time-bombs.   Somebody's
bed is a charred hull, a skeleton.

            Fly away, fly away
home!   What if the portraits
were mine, would I murder
my brothers and sisters?   What if the
ceilings were mine, would I rise
noiseless as helium
and float above the streets?   If the bedroom
were mine, would I become
a nun?   Would I move
to the forest and eat
only black bread and dates?

                    Now
the citizens are comings like insects
to something sweet.   The citizens
stare at the sky, a Niagara of smoke,
the red ashen barber poles whirling.   And the flames
are waving like nightgowns
caught in the wind, the sirens
are shrieking like asylum dreamers,
the smoke mixed with water
eclipses the sun.

Fly away, fly away
home! Somebody's watches are stopped!
Somebody's roses are brittle as wafers!
Somebody's letters curl like snails,
glimmer and writhe like tiny worms!

September 22, 1970

Geoffrey Young

LAURA CHESTER was born April 13, 1949. She grew up in Milwaukee and Oconomowoc, Wisconsin with a large extended family, and she has spent the last few years in New Mexico with her husband, the poet Geoffrey Young. A book of their co-authored poems, *The All Night Salt Lick,* was written while traveling in Africa, published by the Tribal Press, 1972. Her other book of poems is *Tiny Talk,* roundhouse, 1972; *Chunk Off And Float* is ready for publication. She collected an anthology of contemporary poems, *Surprise Sandwiches,* which she uses to teach young people how to write their own poetry. She won the Stelhoff Poetry Prize, and she helps edit *Best Friends* and *Stooge.*

THE HOUSE GUEST

I cannot
write a poem
thin enough
to balance
your huge
horrible presence
in our house
which you moved into
and called your bed.
If I had to watch you
one more morning
bare pot hanging over
red bikini underpants
coming like that to the table
to down some food   coughing
hacked up pieces of sleep.
You slap your stomach
stagger back to bed   yell
Wench   put me on some coffee!
But I don't bring you
the ashtray when you call for it
the one you didn't look for right by your knee.
You tell us that you are sensitive
(to your own basic needs like attention) following
from room to room   we try to get away
but you say   Here   I'll findja poem   Listen to
      this one!
I can't use a poet this important
to himself.   I can't use a poet this fat and proud of it.
Your consuming hulk is eating up what little space we
      have.
There is too much of you to even write a simple subtle
      poem.
You have forced me to write a flabby poem
which I'd sacrifice for one solid blow
right into that hairy gut.
You let me know what a bitch I am.

How could your best friend's wife
treat you like this?   Or your best friend
saying   no offense   nothing personal
but Get Out Today.   We are stunned
when you do.   The curtains fall down
with exhaustion.   Turning off TV
and lights   letting out the smoke
burning the greasy pillowcase
we quietly reclaim our house.
Our house is as nude
as we are   finally
unpossessed.   We
won't send you
our new
address.

HIBERNATING IN
AN OLD LOST NEIGHBORHOOD

CHUNK OFF AND FLOAT   she thought
Make cracks and breathe
again   Dry ice bristles
through hot water   slides away
like tensing reptile hide   knock that
devil up   chopa chopchopchop
Or at least adapt to yourself   she thought
You can thaw out now   come wriggling back
from stiff to steam
but somewhere still
is a frozen nugget of a bird
with its feet stuck together
and its cheee unheard

I can bear any weather imposed   she thought
Come out being more
a woman   call it   puddin in the oven
hot loaves of bread   warmin up the bed
rubber water bottle sloshing

tuck with love
sweaty with comfort and with curves

but who has seen her featherless in snow
cocked head half under   peekaboo
yoohoo   nightflakes like loose tongues
now springing up around her
flakes entranced like bugs around the streetlights
never reach the ground   (time to go now (time
to go home))   Her shoulders   her flimsy dress
the cold doesn't bother her at all

the escape is hers
she knows she's near
she asks strangers for directions home
urgency flashes
a broken lightbulb buzzing
she accepts the generosity of any answer
kicking round in circles
the snow flies up
all too soon she is lost
standing motionless
a stare goes stiff in her eyes   (never find it (never
get back))   She sits down   sinking in
she is going back to sleep again

A WISH FOR WATER

We rise   to comb the fine mist   from our hair
All down to shore   this hour of the morning
sunrise then   the rite begins   with wonder
the couple turns   It's over   We
come alive laughing   Champagne   bubbles in the air
a wonderful way   to go up the stem
the llama says good morning
his breakfast of hydrangeas
We are all in a circle   The water dances
round our legs   The llama milks the flowers

We extend our hands to kiss and be good friends
and love each other daily   We will mend the sky
We will heal each other   Lift off
like leaves   into everything   feels so good
Kick up   This is the morning
of the wedding   sliding by
                                    the light
                on the grass
                        the waves are
                                    flash flash flashin

She sees how it should happen   She will not
disappoint them
                        but her bed now
this lake   is wet with   her hair is
washed back   her ears are
full of tears
and the ache that takes over her body
hurts   like glaciers   giving up
to the change   the melt
gives way to water   She floats   He floats
away

She holds him   over and over
prolonging the dream she wakes from
guilty with feelings   Crush them   No
                        Nurture them
They will be your only children

Holding onto the fact
of her new life   is slippery   as the wet rail fence
she'd cross   going off
alone through fields   away from it all
The high grass   swims
The spider dew   could buoy her   but threads
the web   is easily torn   and every song
sounds sad to her

The sweet champagne   has made her cry
The dance is slow
and graceful   Hands in a circle
so soon broken   makes her cry

They throw her tissue
paper hearts   which flutter in the air   Her heart
would land and melt
there at their feet
                              but she's the bride
They both step in   She's sailing
the water like the body of   her groom
is dying   in her sail like a soft wind
She would have the sail in rags   old
banners   her body
thrown to the waves

She does not look   at the man beside her   owned
but down   for her lover   somewhere in the water
She will sink to him
The songs they sing
from the shore   fall over
her head like a huge sail tipping
Her breath   held back
makes the heart go faster
Her gown   spreads out   like an open rose
His love   dark
like water   rushing around her
carries her down   to home
where his hands will rest upon hers

EYES OF THE GARDEN

for Alice Chester

We have come home here
to be revived by the balm of greenwood and grasses
and the gathering hours in the garden
where feet sink into black earth

and tomatoes are picked sun warmed and in the mout
still warm   where zucchini hair prickles when snappe
from the vine and the swelling bust of summer squash
are arranged in a basket with zinnias.

We come back to this wicker basket to be born again
from the warm potted smell of the green house
into the pace of farmers.
Our days spread out like fields to be grazed
slowly in this August heat.
And yet we are still waiting.
Expectation is a thin honey on our skin.
It's something like the storm's approach
a tense green violet
over the stillness of the water's teal.

We have come home to be cleansed from distance
from speed and the people we passed like mere items
in too many approaches and quick departures.
Relief lies like a wound at the bottom of the lake
where we cry beneath dark waves for the ache
of coming and the ache of going.

Still nourished by communion of summer
the long arms of cousins   the flush on a sister's fac
the hair of a brother   holding onto them for survival.
Back to the oldest woman
who has kept us together like memory.
And now to sit with her and hold her hand
while she diminishes   gazing
like a bouquet of pink and yellow   gazing.

Her skin is of the delicate pansy   her odor of fadi
    roses
but her eyes are delphinium   blue without reserve
so sure of their love   so clear against the slur of day
And when she attaches them to us   we see the ache f
    living

them   that her love is the strength   of shoots
    breaking ground
gain and again.
nd now we have come to watch the flower drop
slowly from her hand
atching that jasmine star to continue.
nd though she is quiet now
know that her eyes are speaking
peaking with the voice of the whole garden.

INDEX

INDEX

405

POETRY FOR ONE AND ALL